GOD'S UNCONDITIONAL *Love*

A Journey!

By
Dr. Helen G. Gilfillan-Farrell

Acknowledgements

I give thanks and honor to God Almighty for granting me the privilege, strength, and courage to embark on this journey and complete the creation of this book.

I am deeply grateful to my adviser, whose inspiration and guidance were invaluable throughout this process. I also extend my heartfelt thanks to those who generously shared their stories and experiences with me.

I wish to express my sincere appreciation to **Ashbery Publishing Co.** for their dedication, professionalism, and support in helping shape this manuscript into its final form. The insight, patience, and commitment displayed have been a tremendous blessing throughout this journey.

Lastly, I express my heartfelt appreciation to my family, relatives, and friends for their unwavering support and encouragement.

Table of Contents

Preface

Welcome to a journey that I hope will shake your core and challenge every preconception you have about love. This book is an emerging tapestry of God's unconditional love, the kind that's relentless and transformative, waiting to pour into every crack and crevice of your heart. Grab your cup of coffee or tea, get comfy, and let's dive into the wild ocean of divine affection together. It's not just a read; it's a call to reflect, unlock, and deepen your connection with love that never stops pursuing you. Seriously, how often do we find ourselves questioning our worthiness of that love? But let me tell you, you are so worthy!

This book isn't just pieced together randomly. Each chapter has been carefully crafted, weaving in personal anecdotes and heartfelt reflections that guide you as you navigate the sometimes rocky terrain of love. Have you ever felt lost while trying to understand how to express love or, even more daunting, how to accept it? You're not alone! As we peel back the layers of each chapter, we'll be exploring the nature of divine love, the way God chases our hearts, and how learning to love fearlessly can change the game in your relationships. Get ready not just to read, but to visualize, feel, and challenge yourself like never before!

Throughout our time together, we'll encounter characters that you might see in a mirror — The Seeker, wrestling with life's questions, and The Mentor, imparting wisdom that resonates deep within. The journey is strategically layered, moving from the essence of God's love directly into practical applications that will stir your heart, blending excitement with profound vulnerability.

I want to stress something crucial: this isn't just about concepts and lofty ideas; we're talking real-life, touchable, actionable love! How can we embody God's love in our daily interactions? What about the sacrifices? Yes, of course we'll explore all that! Think of this as your roadmap to loving not just better but deeper, especially in the communities you're a part of. Hopefully, this one book could take us on such a journey!

And you had better believe that when we wrap our discussions around forgiveness-oh-oh-oh oh, we're going to get real. This isn't just a nice idea; forgiveness has the power to reshape our lives and relationships. We're talking about healing wounds that charm their way into our hearts and shrivel us up if we let them. It's time to step out of the shadows and into the light of love and community! And we will go there, together.

To better understand the hope and assurance that come from God's everlasting love, we will share personal stories and testimonies from people who have experienced it themselves. Their experiences show how God's love can truly change lives. We will hear how the promise of God's love has lifted spirits in times of despair, guided individuals through trials, and ignited a fire of purpose within their souls.

Each chapter will end with reflective questions that are designed to challenge you while nudging you to pause and consider how these lessons can be applied to your life. Because let's face it: we can read all the beautiful words in the world, but if they're not digestible and applicable, what's the point? It's all about transformation — yours, mine, and ours. Together, we can create spaces overflowing with acceptance and love that mirror God's heart.

As we journey through each thematic section, keep in mind, this book isn't just a gathering of thoughts; it's a heartfelt invitation to reflect on your own capacity to love. I can guarantee there will be moments that will bring about emotional reactions, pushing you to reconsider your relationships, your vulnerabilities, and the immense love that is waiting for you to embrace.

I am deeply excited and humbled to share this with you, knowing for sure that each page turned could unlock a new perspective or heal a long-standing hurt. That's my prayer! This is more than literature; it's a movement of love that I hope inspires connections far beyond the pages. So, I encourage you: keep reading! Let these thoughts unravel and ignite a passion for unconditional love within you as we unfold the chapters ahead. Together, let's turn curiosity into discovery and perhaps light the spark that fuels a love revolution in our lives!

With hearts open and minds eager, let's step into this exploration of divine love with genuine excitement and readiness to transform. Let this journey fill your soul as you connect deeper with God's love and your capacity to reflect it back into the world. Here's to the adventure that awaits!

Love and Blessings! Helen

Chapter 1:
The Nature of Divine Love

Understanding Unconditional Love

The concept of unconditional love can often feel abstract, something to be admired rather than experienced. In a world loaded with conditions — expectations, standards, and judgments — it is challenging to grasp the notion of a love that exists without requirement or reservation. Yet, this is precisely the essence of God's love, a love that is freely given, regardless of our shortcomings or failures. To understand unconditional love, we must delve into its core characteristics, as illuminated by biblical references, personal testimonies, and insights from diverse theological perspectives.

At its heart, unconditional love is persistent and relentless. It is a love that does not waver in the face of our struggles, mistakes, or resistance. In Romans 8:38-39, the Apostle Paul assures us that nothing can separate us from the love of God: "For I am convinced that neither death nor life, neither angels nor demons, neither the present nor the future, nor any powers, neither height nor depth, nor anything else in all creation will be able to separate us from the love of God that is in Christ Jesus our Lord." This powerful message reminds us that God's love is present not only in happy or successful times but also during our most difficult and darkest moments. His constant care shows us what it means to have a love that never gives up, no matter what.

The New Testament is rich with stories that exemplify this relentless pursuit of love. Consider the parable of the lost sheep found in Luke 15:3-7. In this account, a shepherd leaves ninety-nine sheep to search for the one that has gone astray. When he finds it, he rejoices with great enthusiasm. This narrative encapsulates the heart of God's love — it is active and dynamic, seeking out those who wander away. The shepherd's actions reflect an unyielding commitment, reminiscent of a parent searching for a lost child, embodying a love that will stop at nothing to bring the lost back into the fold.

Personal testimonies of experiencing God's unconditional love add another layer to our understanding. For instance, take the story of Sarah, a woman in her mid-thirties who struggled with addiction for nearly a decade. Sarah's journey was burdened with pain and guilt, periods of fleeting joy overshadowed by overwhelming shame. When she first encountered God, she couldn't believe that His love could encompass someone like her. Sarah shares the moment of clarity she experienced during a church service when she heard the words, "God loves you just as you are." For Sarah, this realization changed everything. She understood that her past mistakes didn't define her; she was loved as a precious child of God. The love she found wasn't something she had to earn; it was a free gift.

Such testimonies reflect a universal characteristic of divine love: its power to transform. Another powerful story comes from Mark, a former military veteran who faced the demons of PTSD (post-traumatic stress disorder) and depression after returning home. Mark recalls feeling utterly lost and isolated, convinced that no one could understand the depth of his pain. It was during a moment of despair that he encountered a community of believers willing to extend love and support. He recounts how their compassion and unwavering acceptance reminded him of God's love. As he rediscovered faith, Mark felt the shackles of his past begin to loosen. "I didn't have to earn God's love," he explains, "I could just receive it, and that has changed everything."

Mark's experiences echo the message of the gospel, which emphasizes God's readiness to embrace the broken and burdened. Jesus' ministry consistently highlighted the profound depth of God's love for the marginalized and sinful. In John 8:1-11, when a woman caught in adultery was brought before Jesus, He extended grace instead of condemnation. His declaration, "Neither do I condemn you; go and sin no more," embodies the essence of unconditional love. As Jesus interacted with those society deemed unworthy, He illuminated an important truth: love does not require perfection; it demands vulnerability and humility.

This powerful aspect of God's love, its universality, transcends denominational boundaries. Different theological perspectives — all grounded in the central truth of God's love — show a consistent acknowledgment of this unconditional nature. For example, in Catholic doctrine, God's love is considered foundational to the sacramental life, emphasizing the role of grace through the sacraments, which are understood as outward signs of inward grace. The teaching encourages believers to recognize their worth as beloved children of God, irrespective of their failures. The unmerited grace in the sacraments signifies an enduring love that invites transformation each time a believer participates.

Similarly, in Reformed theology, God's sovereign love is often discussed through the lens of election and grace, where believers are not chosen based on merit but out of God's benevolent will. This reflection on grace underscores that we do not earn our place in God's heart; we are welcomed into it. John Calvin famously stated, "There is not a greater blessing than to be embraced by the warmth of divine love." This sentiment illustrates a fundamental principle of Reformed thought — the assurance that God's love pursues us, offering acceptance even in the face of our unworthiness.

As we explore this notion of love, it is important to reflect on our own lives. What barriers do we put up against accepting love, and how does this affect our relationships? The fear of vulnerability can serve as a significant hindrance to the residents of God's love. Consider asking yourself: Are there aspects of your life where you feel unworthy of love? Where do you struggle to allow yourself to be loved unconditionally, either by God or those around you? Reflecting on these barriers opens a pathway to deeper self-awareness and an invitation to experience love at a radically deeper level.

In our quest to understand unconditional love, scripture also presents an image of love that is active rather than passive. James 2:14-17 emphasizes the necessity of faith being accompanied by action, reinforcing that love expresses itself through deeds. This point aligns with the biblical concept of agape love — selfless, sacrificial, and unconditional love that reflects the character of God. Our love should mirror this divine love as we interact with others, extending grace and kindness to those around us, especially to those who may be difficult to love.

Consider the important teaching of Paul in 1 Corinthians 13, which beautifully describes the nature of love: "Love is patient, love is kind. It does not envy, it does not boast, it is not proud. It does not dishonor others, it is not self-seeking, it is not easily angered, and it keeps no record of wrongs." This love is both an action and a choice, one that requires perseverance and compassion. As believers, we are called to embody this love, fostering an environment where grace prevails over judgment and acceptance is prioritized above division.

To move closer to understanding and embodying unconditional love, we should continually ask ourselves how we can be vessels of this divine love in our communities. How can we reflect God's grace in our everyday interactions? What steps can we take to dismantle our preconceived notions about ourselves or others, paving the way for a deeper connection rooted in love?

As we contemplate these questions, it is also essential to recognize that understanding God's unconditional love is a journey, not merely an intellectual exercise but a transformative experience. The more we reflect on our identities as cherished creations, the more likely we are to extend that love outward. Love cannot be contained; it overflows into our actions, shaping our relationships with family, friends, and those on the periphery.

In closing, understanding the depth of God's unconditional love invites us into a transformative relationship with Him and with others. This love is characterized by relentless pursuit, radical acceptance, and tender grace — qualities that transcend human understanding. Through scriptural references, personal testimonies, and theological insights, we begin to see a beautifully solid picture of a love that does not falter, even when we do.

Let us be vessels of this love in our world, breaking down barriers and embracing the call to extend unconditional love in our daily lives. By doing so, we will not only transform ourselves but, importantly, we will contribute to the transformation of those around us. In this sacred act of loving and being loved, we find the true heart of God's divine nature, a nature beckoning us to return love as best we can, and to accept the overwhelming grace that He offers. Reflecting on our own experiences, barriers, and relationships will lead us deeper into the infinite embrace of unconditional love, lighting our path as we journey forward together.

Relentless Nature of God's Love

Just as the sun sinks below the horizon, casting a golden hue over the earth, one cannot help but marvel at the vastness and beauty of creation. Each sunset is a reminder that the day ends, yet the promise of a new dawn lingers on the edge of night. In much the same way, God's love parallels this endless cycle of grace; it is relentless, reaching out to us in every moment of our lives, guiding us through both joy and sorrow.

The beauty of God's love lies in its unyielding nature; it is not dependent on our actions or worthiness. In the Bible, we find numerous stories that reveal the relentless nature of divine love, with the Parable of the Prodigal Son standing out as a magnificent illustration of this truth. Here, we encounter a young man who insists on taking his inheritance and exploring the world, leaving behind the comforts of home and the embrace of his father. As we delve into his journey, we see how the son squanders his riches on reckless living, finding himself lost and broken in a foreign land.

Amidst the grime of his choices, the image of his father holding the door open to hope emerges. The father, representing God's relentless love, does not stand idly by but, instead, waits faithfully, looking for the return of his wayward son. How heart-wrenching it is to imagine the father's days filled with longing, his hope unwavering despite every poor decision made by the son. When at last the son returns, burdened with guilt and shame weighing heavily upon him, it is the father who runs to greet him. This passionate embrace is not merely a reflection of familial affection but a vivid depiction of God's love relentlessly pursuing each of us, regardless of our failures.

In the moment of reunion, the father does not scold or express disappointment. Instead, he celebrates the return of his son, placing a robe on his shoulders, a ring on his finger, and sandals on his feet. This is a lavish display of love and acceptance, a symbolic demonstration that there is nothing we can do to strip away our identity as beloved children of God. This story invites us to recall that God's love pursues us in our most unlovable states, assuring us that no depth of sin or despair can deter His desire to fully embrace us.

However, the relentless pursuit of God's love does not stop at a single story from Scripture; it continues to weave through the lives of countless individuals who have encountered the transformative power of this love. Let us consider the story of Elsie, a woman who faced her share of setbacks and struggles. After a painful divorce, she found herself lost, grappling not only with feelings of rejection but questions of worth. In the depths of her despair, Elsie attended a local church, encouraged by a friend who insisted the community would be embracing. Reluctantly, she entered a space that felt foreign, where love was supposed to abound.

At first, Elsie felt invisible among the congregation, her heart wrapped in fear and uncertainty. Yet, the very essence of this community was a reflection of the relentless love of God. The warmth of smiles, the authenticity of shared stories, and the sincerity of genuine welcome slowly chipped away at the walls she had built around her heart. Over time, she encountered individuals who shared their journeys of brokenness and redemption, revealing how God's love had pursued them during their own moments of desperation.

Then came a defining event: the church held a prayer night for those who longed for healing. In that sacred space, surrounded by strangers who had become friends, Elsie unleashed the turmoil she had tightly held. As tears cascaded down her face, she felt an unexpected release. In that passionate moment, something shifted within; she experienced the relentless embrace of God's love — a love that wrapped her in acceptance and hope, whispering promises of renewal amid her uncertainties.

Like Elsie, there are others who have felt the relentless nature of God's love intersecting with their lives in powerful and transformative ways. Take David, for example. Raised in a loving environment, he, too, faced challenges as he grew. The pressures of societal expectations and personal ambitions led to a season of estrangement from God. In those dark days, David made choices that veered off course; he succumbed to a lifestyle of superficiality that left him feeling increasingly hollow.

One day, in the midst of a gathering with friends fueled by laughter and revelry, David experienced an unexpected moment of clarity. Despite the intoxication all around him, he felt an inner emptiness, a constant pain that persisted beneath the surface of the facade of joy.

As he left that party feeling desolate, he found himself overwhelmed by memories of a childhood spent in the warmth of faith and understanding of God's unending love. It was as though a voice whispered gently to him, urging him to return home — a home defined not by a physical location but by the heart of a loving Father who never ceases to seek us out.

That night marked a turning point for David. He decided to reach out to a childhood friend who had remained steadfast in his faith. Their conversation turned into a beautiful reminder that God's love always offers us an invitation to return, regardless of how far we might have strayed. David's journey back to faith was not quick, nor was it without its challenges. Yet day by day, he rediscovered the relentless love of God enveloping him, reminding him that he was never truly lost.

As David's story unfolds, we see another layer of the relentless nature of God's love revealed: the love that pursues us, that offers redemption and healing even in our brokenness. God's love not only finds the lost but also carries us when we are too weary to walk back on our own. This is the essence of grace, pouring over our mistakes, allowing us to step into new possibilities, and making us whole again.

Scripture is full of verses reminding us of this unwavering affection. Romans 8:38-39 declares that nothing can separate us from the love of God — not death, nor life, nor angels, nor demons, nor anything else in all creation. This proclamation is crafted to soothe our anxieties and remind us that the divine love we receive does not fade with our failings or frustrations. It is not contingent upon our performance or compliance with rules. Through the diverse narratives of God's people — from ancient times to our contemporary lives — this truth reverberates through history: God's love relentlessly seeks, finds, heals, and restores.

This relentless pursuit mirrors the imagery found in the natural world — a world where each creature, every heartbeat, resonates with the divine rhythm of love. Consider the mighty ocean with its waves that crash persistently upon the shore, never ceasing, always returning. Or the rivers that carve their way through the rigid earth, gradually but surely finding their path to reunite with the sea. God's love behaves similarly; it is forceful, healing, and persistent.

As we engage with the stories of others who have walked through shadows only to emerge into light, we begin to cultivate a deeper appreciation for the relentless nature of God's love in our own lives. Like the Prodigal Son, we may wander, but the grace of a loving Father awaits us, longing to encircle us in a reunion filled with joy and celebration. Our struggles, our doubts, our failures — all moments that prove our humanity — serve only to demonstrate the profound depth of God's love waiting on the other side.

Moreover, this relentless love is not meant solely for our benefit. Just as we are recipients of divine grace, we are also called to reflect this love to those around us. In doing so, we fulfill our purpose as vessels of God's affection, illuminating the lives of those who feel lost and alone in this vast world. The story of Elsie continues to inspire as she shares her journey, encouraging others to embrace vulnerability. Now a pillar of support in her community, she draws from her own experience to remind others of the hope that lies in being loved unconditionally.

Let us also not forget David, who now actively shares his journey of repentance and renewal. His story resonates with those grappling with their own battles, offering consolation to those who may feel unworthy of love. Through his authenticity and the healing power of vulnerability, David fosters a culture of belonging rooted in God's relentless love — a love that transcends judgment and celebrates redemption.

Ultimately, the relentless nature of God's love beckons us to reflect deeply on our relationships, both with ourselves and with others. It challenges us to cultivate an understanding of what it means to love without conditions, free of judgment, grounded in acceptance. As we become aware of our own need for compassion and grace, we begin to embody that love in tangible ways.

This exploration of God's relentless love invites us into a dance of grace — a rhythm that pulses through all living things and places an eternal longing within our hearts. How have we mirrored this relentless love in our relationships? Where have we felt the gentle hands of love lifting us from our despair? As we uncover these layers, an awakening occurs within us — a realization that we are loved without measure.

As we engage with the relentless nature of God's love, let us rethink our pathways, our wanderings, and our return to the embrace of belonging. In moments of struggle and uncertainty, may we cling to the truth that we are passionately pursued, ever loved, and unconditionally received, just as we are.

In this exploration of God's profound and relentless love, may we find solace in the knowledge that we are always welcome home, and may we extend that same love to illuminate the world around us. In every heartbeat and every motion, the vastness of divine affection calls to us: we are not alone; we are endlessly loved.

The Journey to Understanding Love

Towards the dusk of the evening, the sun casting a warm golden glow over the fields, the Seeker sat on a wooden bench, his heart heavy with questions. The air was thick with the scent of freshly bloomed flowers, yet all he could feel was a sense of longing, of grappling with a truth that eluded him. He was a wanderer of spirit, yearning to understand the nature of love, particularly the divine love that so many spoke about, yet few seemed to truly comprehend.

"Why is love so difficult to accept?" he murmured to the wind, half hoping for an answer. His journey had taken him through winding paths of heartache, confusion, and fleeting glimpses of affection, yet still, he found himself lost in contemplation. Today, he felt particularly distant from that love, as if it were a foreign concept belonging to a different realm.

Then came the soft rustle of leaves as the Mentor approached, her presence displayed warmth and understanding. Taking a seat beside him, she smiled gently. "It seems you're deep in thought today, my friend."

"I am," the Seeker replied, releasing a heavy sigh. "It's just… love. I see it everywhere, hear about it in songs and sermons, but what is it really? Why do I struggle so much to believe that I am worthy of it?"

"Ah, the struggle to understand love," the Mentor nodded knowingly. "You are not alone in this journey. Many have walked this path before you, tangled in the weeds of mistrust and societal expectations."

"But how do I find my way out?" he pleaded, his voice marked with desperation. "How do I move past these doubts and truly understand the essence of divine love?"

The Mentor paused, allowing his words to sink in. "Let's explore that together. Often, our understanding of love becomes clouded by the weight of expectation, both from society and ourselves. You've been conditioned to believe that love must be earned, that it comes with conditions. But divine love? It is given freely and unconditionally."

As the Seeker absorbed her words, images began to flood his mind — moments of joy when he felt loved and equally moments of heartache when he felt undeserving. "But what does it mean to receive love without reservation?" he asked, curiosity mixed with skepticism.

"Imagine a river," the Mentor suggested. "It flows tirelessly, regardless of the terrain it crosses, nourishing everything in its path. Divine love operates in a similar fashion. It flows abundantly, seeking us out even when we hide or turn away. The challenge lies not in the love itself, but in our ability to receive it."

"But why do I struggle so much with receiving?" the Seeker reflected aloud, grappling with his own introspective thoughts. "I find myself holding back... afraid of what it truly means. It seems safer to keep love at arm's length."

"Fear can be a powerful barrier," the Mentor observed. "What is it that you fear?"

"I fear vulnerability," he admitted slowly. "To accept love means to open oneself up to the possibility of pain, rejection. I've experienced that before, and it hurt deeply. Sometimes I wonder if I'm even deserving of love in the first place."

"Your worthiness is not determined by past pain or rejection," she gently reminded him. "Divine love is as radical as it is boundless; it does not ask for perfection, only willingness. We often forget that God's love does not hinge on our ability to earn it. It exists simply because it wants to. Just like that river, it nurtures even the most barren lands."

The Seeker contemplated the metaphor, realizing that in his heart, he had always viewed love as a transaction. "I suppose I've always believed that to truly deserve love, I needed to achieve something remarkable or be someone I'm not," he murmured. "But maybe... just maybe... that's where I've gone wrong."

"Accepting that you are enough as you are, is a crucial step," the Mentor encouraged. "Think of the times you've loved — was it conditional? Did you love someone because they were perfect or met certain criteria?"

"No," he answered, surprised by the clarity of his own thoughts. "I've loved deeply, flaws and all, accepting people as they are."

"Exactly. And if you can extend that grace to others, why not to yourself?" she challenged gently, her gaze unwavering. "Divine love invites you to witness that same acceptance extended to you."

A flicker of understanding ignited within the Seeker. "So, I need to change the narrative in my mind?"

The Mentor nodded. "Yes. Shift from an understanding of love rooted in performance to one grounded in grace. The divine pursuit of love is relentless; it seeks, it forgives, it embraces. When you allow yourself to feel this, to truly accept it, you will begin to view love through a different lens."

"But how do I dismantle the societal expectations that have shaped my understanding?" he questioned, feeling the weight of the world pressing against him.

"Start by recognizing the lies you've believed," she said. "Many of us carry notions that we must be successful, attractive, or perfect to be deserving of love. Society teaches us that vulnerability is weakness, but the truth is that vulnerability is the birthplace of connection. Ask yourself: How have these beliefs served you, and at what cost?"

As the Seeker pondered her question, a floodgate of emotions washed over him. He realized how much he had held back for fear of judgment — that he had erected walls, not just against pain but against the love that could have filled those spaces. "I've built those walls so high, I didn't even realize how lonely I had become," he confessed. "It's exhausting to feel disconnected."

"Loneliness often masks itself as self-protection," the Mentor replied softly. "But true love can only flourish in openness. It is a delicate dance, and there will be times of hurt. Yet, remember the joy, the freedom, the authenticity found in embracing it."

With each passing moment, the Seeker felt as if he was peeling away layers of fear and doubt, exposing a fragile yet hopeful heart. "How do I begin to dismantle those barriers?" he asked, eager to take the first steps.

"Start small," the Mentor suggested. "Practice accepting love in its many forms — an encouraging word, a smile from a stranger, the kindness of a friend. Allow yourself to receive the love that surrounds you daily. Notice how that feels. You may just find that love is closer than you imagined."

He nodded slowly, absorbing her wisdom but still a bit doubtful. "But are these small acts enough? How can I be sure?"

"Trust the process," she said, placing a comforting hand on his shoulder. "The journey to understanding love is not measured by grand gestures but by the integrity of our hearts. It's the sincerity with which we choose to connect that makes love profound. Reflect on the places where you've seen love's impact — how it transformed your relationships, your perspective."

For the first time, the Seeker glanced at the world around him with a renewed sense of focus. Another question emerged; this one felt more intense. "What role does grace play in this journey?"

"Grace is the thread that binds love and acceptance. It is what allows us to approach love without fear of judgment," the Mentor explained. "It invites you to forgive not just others but yourself. When you acknowledge your imperfections and allow yourself grace, love becomes a sanctuary rather than a battleground."

"I've never thought about it like that," he admitted, curiosity arousing within him. "If I embrace grace, does that mean I also allow myself to forgive those who have wronged me?"

"Precisely," the Mentor affirmed. "Forgiveness is liberating; it unchains you from the past. It allows you to view love with a clean slate, unencumbered by resentment or bitterness. In this way, you can foster a deeper connection with both God and others."

The Seeker contemplated that idea, imagining how forgiveness could open new pathways in his heart. "But it feels so unsettling— release; it seems as though the wounds are too deep."

"It can be daunting, but remember, forgiveness does not erase the pain; it transforms it. As you learn to forgive both yourself and others, you're inviting healing into your life," the Mentor reassured him. "It is a journey, and each small step you take matters. With each embrace of grace, each act of kindness, love becomes less foreign."

"Where do I begin?" he asked, in a softer tone now, as if the weight started lifting just a bit.

"Embrace the whispers of love in your life. Start with gratitude, acknowledge the moments when you feel loved, no matter how small. Reflect on instances where you've experienced grace, and allow that to guide your journey. Love is often found in the ordinary."

As the sun sank lower, the warm shades of twilight surrounded the two figures on the bench, casting long shadows across the field. A new realization blossomed within the Seeker, a gentle acceptance that understanding love was a journey, not a destination. There was no direct path, only the willingness to explore, to ask, and to listen.

"Thank you," he breathed, feeling a spark of hope ignite within. "I think I'm beginning to see it is about more than just the destination. It's about the willingness to engage, to confront fears, and to open my heart to the possibility of love."

The Mentor smiled, a glimmer of pride in her eyes. "Your journey has already started, my friend. Embrace the journey, for it will be one of the most profound and rewarding experiences you'll encounter."

The Seeker lingered on her words as the shadows lengthened, feeling a renewed sense of purpose swell within him. He understood now that his journey was not solitary; it was a shared experience with a community of fellow seekers, each grappling with their own doubts, fears, and discoveries along the way.

With a heart a little lighter and courage gently nudging him forward, the Seeker stood up. "I think I'm ready for this journey, to seek love, to embrace grace, and to let go of my fears. It may not be easy, but I believe it will be worth it."

"Indeed, it will."   The Mentor nodded as she stood beside him. "Remember, every step you take toward understanding love is precious. Each moment spent in reflection, each connection made, this is where true love resides. Trust in the journey, trust in the love that surrounds you, and trust in yourself."

As they walked together through the tranquil scenery, the Seeker felt a quiet determination blossom within him. The road ahead was uncertain and filled with potential hardships, but for the first time, he felt hopeful. God's love, wild and unrelenting, was there waiting for him, ready to meet him in all his messiness, his imperfections.

And in that moment, as they strolled through the golden light, he knew the journey to understanding love was not just about finding the answer. It was about exploring, questioning, and continuously opening oneself to the overwhelming, never-ending embrace of a love that was always there.

Chapter 2:
Chasing the Lost

The Parable of the Lost Sheep

In a peaceful region scattered with rolling hills and overrun with wildflowers, nightfall began to darken the scenery. The air was sweet with the scent of grass and earth, as the sun almost lowered toward the horizon. A soft rustling echoed through the fields, interrupted by the fading bleats of sheep winding their way back to the fold. Among them roamed a shepherd, his roughened hands and sun-burned face revealing a life devoted to tending his flock. His heart was a compilation of stories — each sheep, precious to his soul.

Yet, as the shepherd counted his flock, a pang of anxiety pierced his heart. One sheep was missing. The shepherd felt the panic in his mind, unbelievable. The familiar sound of bleating was now overshadowed by an unsettling silence, echoing deeper than the emptiness of the paddock. He glanced around, scanning the distance. The sheep that had strayed was not just a number; it was a cherished soul; one he loved just as fiercely as the others.

This is where we find our protagonist — the shepherd. The parable of the lost sheep transcends time and culture, resonating deeply within the hearts of those who hear it. It is a story embedded in the folds of biblical teachings, spoken by Jesus Himself, and designed to illustrate the depth of God's love for His creation, particularly for those who find themselves wandering away from the safety of His embrace.

As the last rays of the sun bowed out, the shepherd stood resolute. He would not return home without the lost one. His heart ached to think of the vulnerability faced by the sheep on its own, wandering through the unknown. Perhaps it had been led astray by a fleeting temptation — a patch of greener grass that seemed irresistible but was likely loaded with danger. This, perhaps, is how we often find ourselves lost in our journeys of faith or relationships, lured by the prospect of joy, only to encounter shadows lurking in the folds of our choices.

So, the shepherd took a deep breath, filled with a blend of determination and trepidation, and stepped into the encroaching darkness of the woods. Each step was a mix of hope and fear, mirroring the emotions we experience when we search for someone or something lost. Would he find his precious sheep? Would it be injured, weary, or frightened? The uncertainty appeared larger than the trees around him.

As he made his way through the mass of bushes and plants, memories echoed in his mind: the first time he had brought each sheep into the fold, the laughter that danced through the air as they played under the watchful eye of the sun. The shepherd's love for his flock was not contingent on their behavior; he loved them simply because they belonged to him. Likewise, God's love for each of us does not diminish based on our decisions or our distance from Him. His heart aches for every lost soul, longing for their return to the warmth of His embrace.

With each passing moment, the shepherd called out to the lost sheep, his voice echoing softly through the stillness of the night. "Come back, my dear!" he pleaded, his tone filled with both authority and tenderness. "You are cherished! You are missed! I will not forsake you!" As shadows danced around him, each rustle of leaves brought a flicker of hope, urging him onward through the uncertainty.

Life often presents us with moments where we feel lost — lost in our faith, in our relationships, and sometimes even in our very identity. The feeling can be overwhelming, like wandering through a thick fog where all familiar landmarks have disappeared. It is in these moments of darkness that we may find ourselves questioning: Am I still loved? Do I still belong?

The lost sheep reflected this desperation. It had strayed too far from the fold, grazing idly, unaware of the distance it had created between itself and the safety of the shepherd's watchful care. Fear brewed within its heart, a cyclone of anxiety over the unknown. Every rustle turned into a boogeyman; every sound a reminder of its isolation. In its desperate search for something that seemed better, the sheep only found the cold embrace of solitude and uncertainty.

Just as the shepherd is relentless in his pursuit, God, too, seeks us earnestly. His heart aches for us not only because of the distance created by our actions but also because of the very nature of what it means to be lost — lost in doubt, lost in pain, lost in despair. The overwhelming longing that the shepherd feels encompasses that same yearning found in our Creator. He treasures us as individuals, constantly ready to welcome us back into the fold, to embrace us despite our wounds and flaws.

Finally, the shepherd's perseverance bore fruit. As he came around a bend, a faint bleating emerged from the distance, trembling and vulnerable. His heart leaped; a rush of adrenaline propelled him forward. There, nestled among the thickets, the lost sheep stood, unsure and frightened. Relief flooded the shepherd when he laid eyes on that precious creature; love outweighed the exhaustion of the search. With a heart full of compassion, he knelt beside the trembling sheep. "I've come for you," he whispered, gently brushing his fingers through its wool, infusing it with the warmth of comfort and safety.

In that moment, the emotional turmoil of both the shepherd and the sheep collided. The shepherd's relief transformed into joy and delight as he scooped the sheep into his arms, holding it close to his heart. It was no longer lost; it had been found, and the joy that erupted within him was unparalleled. This reunion evokes the very essence of God's love for us — the moment we turn back towards Him, despite the roads we've traveled away from grace.

Together, they began the journey home, one step at a time, as the stars emerged in the night sky. The shepherd's spirit radiated with joy, reflecting the clarity of purpose reignited within him. In the love of the shepherd, we are reminded that our losses, whether physical or spiritual, are never beyond the reach of God's grace. His passion fuels pursuit; His heart never rests as He longs for our return.

As he carried the sheep back to the fold, the shepherd could finally see the familiar horizon glimmering in the distance. There was strength in his stride and hope in his heart. The lost sheep, nestled safely in his arms, bore witness to the unfathomable grace that accompanies true love. Furthermore, as the shepherd crossed the threshold of his fold, a chorus of joyful bleats erupted from the awaiting flock, welcoming their lost companion back into the warmth of community.

Being lost in life can often leave us wrestling with shame and self-doubt. It can gnaw at our spirits like a relentless predator, whispering untruths that lead us to believe we are undeserving of love and acceptance. But the parable of the lost sheep beckons us to a place of divine truth: there exists a love that transcends our failures and embraces our imperfections. It is a love that relentlessly seeks out and finds us, no matter how far we may stray.

This story culminates in an invitation for reflection. Have you ever felt lost in your faith, struggling to find your way back to God? Perhaps there have been moments when the shadows loomed too large, overshadowing the light of hope. Take a moment to consider how God sees you — an individual of immeasurable worth, someone He actively pursues. His grace is readily available, and just as the shepherd searched for his lost sheep, He is continually calling out for you.

Consider the times of your own wandering, and how they may have shaped your experiences. What led to your straying? Was it an emotional longing for something you thought was missing in your life? Perhaps relationships soured, or doubts began to seed themselves in your heart. Whatever the reasons, know that each one is met with compassion in the eyes of our Creator. He understands our struggles; He empathizes with our pain. He waits for us patiently, yearning for us to recognize His presence.

As we arrive at the parable's conclusion, we are left with application. Reflect on the love we are called to embody, just as the shepherd did. How can we reflect that same persistence in our relationships with others? Are there loved ones in your life who have strayed, who may need your heart's earnest pursuit to guide them back home?

In a world where isolation is rampant, consider how you might be a beacon of hope for those lost in their own darkness, encouraging them to see the light of love's embrace, and igniting within them the invitation to return. As community is a vital part of belonging, nurturing love and compassion becomes our challenge — through every act, big or small, we can remind others that they are indeed cherished and never lost to the gaze of divine love.

The parable of the lost sheep is a vivid illustration of the unconditional love God has for humanity. It serves as a reminder that no one is beyond reach, that we are all worthy of pursuit, and that the heart of God beats with relentless grace for every wandering soul. As we reflect on our own journeys, may we find comfort in knowing that, regardless of the paths we take, there is always a shepherd waiting to carry us home.

Personal Stories of Being Found

The air was thick with uncertainty, a heavy weight that pressed down upon Mildred's chest. She looked around the darkened room, where shadows shifted on the walls, mirroring her inner conflict. She was engulfed in a seemingly limitless emptiness, as if she had created the storm herself. The walls of her life had been closing in, and with each passing moment, she felt more lost than ever. It was a period marked by despair — job loss, a failed relationship, and a deep sense of disconnection from her faith. Mildred was wrestling with doubts, questions that seemed too vast to articulate. How had she strayed so far? Where was the light?

In the midst of her turmoil, an unexpected moment changed everything. One night, feeling utterly defeated, Mildred found herself wandering aimlessly through the streets of her town. The chill in the air was much like the coldness in her heart. It was then that she heard a gentle voice — a friend's call from across the street. It was Mary, a woman from her church, who had always embodied warmth and kindness. Their eyes met, and without hesitation, Mary crossed over, embracing Mildred in a tight hug. It was in that moment, wrapped in the love of a friend, that Mildred felt a flicker of hope rekindle within her.

Mary invited Mildred to join her for prayers that night at the church. Hesitant at first, Mildred felt a tug at her heart — something deep inside urged her to go. As they entered the familiar space, the echoes of worship music grasped them, soothing Mildred's troubled spirit. The sanctuary, once a place she had taken for granted, became her refuge. As the congregation sang, Mildred allowed herself to be vulnerable; the tears streamed down her face.

In that sacred space, surrounded by people who shared their stories of struggle and grace, Mildred felt something shift within her. She felt found. The unconditional love displayed by her community reminded her that she was not alone. As she reflected on her own pain, she realized that God had been present through it all. Even in her darkest days, He had never abandoned her.

Mike's journey began in the depths of addiction. For years, he had been shackled by a substance that promised freedom but instead left him in bondage. Every day was a battle, and he felt like a ghost wandering the streets — isolated, ashamed, and lost. Family and friends had given up hope, and he had long given up on himself. But amidst the chaos of his life, there came a moment — a simple invitation to attend a recovery group meeting led by a former addict who had found redemption in faith.

Reluctantly, Mike walked into the room, skeptical and apprehensive. The faces in the circle told stories of struggle that mirrored his own, and for the first time, he felt seen. As he listened, something began to shift deep within his heart. One of the speakers shared about the love of God, a love that pursued even those who had run farthest away. It was a never-failing love that sought the lost, just as the shepherd sought his lost sheep. Mike felt a spark of realization: he was that lost sheep.

That night, as he sat among his newfound friends, he experienced a sense of belonging that had long eluded him. In sharing their struggles, they became a tapestry of hope woven together by the threads of divine love. Mike left that meeting knowing he was not beyond redemption, that being found was possible. For the first time in years, he had hope — a feeling that God was pursuing him, even in his darkest moments.

Jennifer's story unfolded in the aftermath of a devastating loss. The sudden passing of her father left her grappling with grief that felt insurmountable. Questions of "Why?" and "What now?" swirled in her mind, and the numbness settled in, making life feel like an endless fog. Friends attempted to offer comfort, but the ache in her heart felt like a chasm that separated her from everything she once cherished.

One Saturday, as she sat in a park, trying to catch a glimpse of sunlight through the clouds, an elderly woman approached her. Recognizing her distress, the woman sat down beside her and spoke gently. "I lost my husband last year," she said, her eyes revealing a depth of understanding. As they shared their stories, Jennifer found solace in the connection forged through pain. The woman spoke about how her journey had led her to a place of deeper faith and reliance on God, the very foundation that had felt like it was crumbling beneath her feet.

As their conversation unfolded, Jennifer felt the warmth of God's presence through this stranger. The elderly woman prayed for her right there under the streaks of sunlight. In the intimate act of prayer, Jennifer felt and sensed the divine love enveloping her, assuring her that she was not alone in her grief. She realized that God's love often manifests through others, creating connections that help us navigate our darkest valleys.

Each of these stories weaves into a larger narrative of the human experience: the struggle to find our way back, the longing to be 'found' by a loving God. Every person, in their own unique journey, has stories that reflect their search for belonging and understanding. Whether it is Mildred in her moment of vulnerability, Mike in his battle against addiction, or Jennifer in her grief, each encounter with divine love serves as a reminder that God relentlessly pursues His children.

Joanne, a single mother, often wrestled with feelings of inadequacy. Balancing work, parenting, and her own spiritual life felt like an uphill struggle. One particularly challenging week, overwhelmed by work obligations and her child's needs, she broke down. In her frantic moment, she turned to prayer, questioning how she could possibly be the mother her child needed while feeling so utterly lost herself.

That Sunday, during the sermon, the pastor spoke on the importance of community and how God's love fills the gaps we cannot. As he asked everyone to share their struggles, tears filled Joanne's eyes when another mother shared her own burdens — a reflection of Joanne's own fear and worry. It was in this vulnerable moment that Joanne realized she was not alone. The love of God, through the virtual embrace of the church community, began to mend the broken pieces of her heart.

After the service, as she spoke with the other mothers, a transformative connection emerged. Their empathy and understanding provided both comfort and strength. Joanne no longer felt the weight of her struggles alone; the love of God flowed through these friendships, fortifying her spirit for the challenges ahead.

As each story unfolds, we see how being 'found' often comes through the unexpected hands of others — through friends, support groups, casual encounters, or shared struggles. These moments of connection remind us that God's love is far-reaching and decisive, manifesting through both intimate moments and grand gestures.

James's story is a powerful testament to this truth. A veteran who returned from war, burdened with trauma, found himself without purpose. He settled into a daily existence devoid of joy, feeling lost amidst the noise of the world. One day, he reluctantly accompanied a friend to a service event at a local community center. Resigned to just going through the motions, he didn't anticipate the impact it would have on him.

As he volunteered, he interacted with those who, like him, felt displaced. Listening to their stories, he felt an undeniable shift within himself. In serving others, he started to unravel the layers of despair that had been holding him captive. The spark of purpose reignited within him, and he recognized that his experiences, however painful, could guide him to serve those who were suffering.

Through this new community, James felt God's presence guiding him each step of the way. He transitioned from being lost in his struggles to rediscovering a sense of direction, finding purpose in serving those who were also seeking to be 'found.' Each face he encountered reflected a piece of his own journey, bringing him a profound sense of connection and the sweetness of shared pain.

These personal narratives illuminate the truth that we are not alone in our struggles. Through the ups and downs of life, God remains an ever-present force, inviting us to experience His love through one another. As we consider these stories, we can foster a greater understanding that within our own darkness lies the potential for transformation, not only for ourselves but for those we encounter. When we recall our moments of feeling 'lost,' we can also think of our moments of being 'found.' Maybe it was the neighbor who provided a timely meal, a friend who stayed up late to listen, or a brief exchange with a stranger that shifted our perspective. These appear as threads in a great masterpiece designed to illustrate the unwavering grace that enfolds our lives.

As we embrace our shared humanity, we recognize that God's love transcends our personal experiences, merging them into a collective narrative of seeking and being sought. Through acknowledging these stories, we bridge gaps between our lives, illustrating the beauty of divine love in its many forms. This communal journey of faith invites us all to recognize when we have been found and informs us how we, in turn, can help others find their way.

Each narrative in this subchapter leads us back to the same conclusion: God loves the lost, and we brilliantly express that love through our interactions with one another. The world may often feel isolating and cold, but these stories remind us that the heart of God beats powerfully through the bonds we form with one another.

In moments of being 'lost,' may we come to embrace our vulnerability, welcoming the warmth of our community. And in moments of being 'found,' let us be mindful of the responsibility we carry to uplift others who may still be on their journey. Reflect on your experiences as you embrace this truth: we are all threads in the fabric of divine love, woven together through the pursuit of grace and understanding.

Through sharing our stories, we not only find healing but also empower others to see their paths illuminated by love. In the collective experience of being found, we embody the relentless chase of God's love that invites everyone into the fold — a community where no one stands alone, and all are celebrated as beloved children of the Most High.

Reflection and Practical Application

As we conclude our exploration of what it means to be chased by God's love, it is essential to take a moment for reflection and practical application. Love is a profound theme that resonates deeply within us, inviting us to analyze our own journeys in the light of divine affection. The narratives of being lost and found evoke feelings that are universally human, and it is through these feelings that we find our connection to God's relentless pursuit.

To begin this reflective process, I invite you to pause and reflect on your own experiences of love — both the times when you felt cherished and whole, and the moments when you felt lost, isolated, or unworthy. Think of these experiences as pieces of a puzzle that, when put together, create a fuller picture of who you are and how you relate to the divine.

Consider the following questions to guide your reflections:

1. When in your life did you feel most distant from God? What contributed to that feeling of separation?
2. Describe a moment when you felt God's love chasing after you. What did that experience look like, and how did it make you feel?
3. How have your past experiences shaped your understanding of God's love and acceptance? Are there specific incidents that stand out to you?
4. What does being 'lost' mean to you personally? How do you recognize when you are in a state of feeling lost?
5. Reflect on the idea of being found. Have there been individuals or moments in your life that served as catalysts for bringing you back to a place of faith, hope, or belonging? Who were they, and how did they impact you?

After you've had the chance to ponder these questions, let's explore some practical applications that can help ground your insights in actionable steps. The relationship between divine love and our responses within our communities is crucial. Recognizing that we, too, can be instruments of God's love is a powerful realization — one that calls us to be active participants in sharing that love with others.

1. **Connecting with Others:** Reflect on those around you — friends, family, colleagues, or even acquaintances. Who might be feeling lost or in need of an uplifting word or gesture? This week, make it a point to reach out to one person in particular. This could be a simple text message, phone call, or an in-person visit. Share a moment of kindness with them, reminding them that they are loved and valued.
2. **Creating Safe Spaces:** Consider ways you can facilitate an environment of love and acceptance in your spaces — be it at home, in the workplace, at church, or within your community. This could involve starting a conversation about struggles with faith or loneliness, ensuring to listen and provide understanding when others share their

feelings. Lead by example in creating a culture where vulnerability is cherished and love is freely expressed.

3. **Community Involvement:** Engage in community service or outreach programs that resonate with your passion and values. Whether volunteering at a local community center, participating in mentorship programs, or taking part in charity events, these acts embody the love we've received from God. It not only impacts those in need but also strengthens your sense of belonging to a community that shares the goal of chasing the lost with God's love.

4. **Journaling Your Journey:** Create a dedicated space in your journal titled "Lost and Found." Write freely about the moments from your life when you felt lost, identifying the emotions and thoughts that accompanied these times. Next, balance this by documenting the times you felt found — what realizations, people, or divine interventions brought you back to a place of love? Allow this exercise to serve as both a reflective practice and a source of inspiration, celebrating the many facets of your spiritual journey.

5. **Pray and Meditate:** Incorporate a daily practice of prayer and meditation that focuses on God's love. When you pray, ask God to reveal ways in which you can reach out to others who may be feeling lost. Meditate on scriptures that emphasize God's relentless pursuit and love. Let these scriptures sink deeply into your heart. Reflect on how you can live out this love in practical terms each day.

6. **Cultivating Openness:** As you gain confidence in sharing love and kindness with others, consider what it means to be on the receiving end of love. Are there areas in your life where you struggle to accept love from others or God? Contemplate how opening your heart to loving and being loved can create transformative experiences. Talk to someone you trust about your hesitations and let them support you in this journey toward vulnerability.

Remember that love is not only meant for us to receive but also to extend actively. Whether we're aware of it or not, every interaction has the potential to reflect the divine love we've encountered. The Mentor reminds us gently that to love others is to show them a path toward healing and wholeness, much like the path we ourselves have traveled. Each small step we take in sharing love serves to foster hope and security for those around us.

As you engage with these reflective questions and actions, it is vital to remember that you are not alone in this journey. Just as God actively pursues those who feel lost, you are surrounded by a community of individuals who equally yearn for connection and understanding. Your willingness to share your love, paired with the awareness of how God's love has sought you, creates a ripple effect that can change lives.

In conclusion, let this serve as a call to action — one that highlights the beauty of love shared within a community and the importance of never underestimating your ability to impact someone's life positively. Each kind word, every thoughtful action, and all instances of shared vulnerability pave the way for healing and hope. As you reflect on and embody God's relentless love, let it compel you to chase after the lost, revealing the richness that life can hold when infused with love and grace. Embrace this journey with courage, knowing that as you turn outward to love others, you draw ever closer to the heart of God.

Chapter 3:
The Extravagant Love

Understanding Extravagant Love

Extravagant love is a term that may initially sound excessive, even unsettling. In a world where love is often defined by safety, reciprocity, and boundaries, how can we reconcile such a bold declaration? To call love "extravagant" means it gives freely and without limits, offers without expecting anything in return, and has the courage to go where common sense might warn us not to. This chapter will go through what extravagant love truly means, examining its complexities and implications through biblical insights and real-life reflections.

At its core, extravagant love is an expression of unreserved passion. It refuses to be hindered by fear of vulnerability or rejection. Consider the story of the Good Samaritan, which demonstrates how powerful love can be when it transcends social rules and divisions. In the parable, Jesus speaks of a Samaritan who, though marginalized by his culture, stops to help a wounded stranger. He risks judgment and even personal safety to do what is right. This encounter is a quintessential portrayal of extravagant love; it defies social hierarchies and embraces vulnerability out of sheer compassion.

To embrace extravagant love is to recognize the transformative power it holds, not only for those who receive it but also for those who give it. The Bible abounds with examples of God's immeasurable love for humanity. It begins in Genesis, where God creates a world of beauty and abundance. Later, in the New Testament, we see the greatest expression of love when Jesus gives His life on the cross. Throughout Scripture, this kind of lavish, selfless love is a constant theme. This love is extravagant, immeasurable, and unfathomable.

Yet, embracing such love is not without its challenges. The Seeker, representing anyone striving to comprehend or embody this kind of love, often wrestles with personal doubts and fears. What does it mean to love without limits? What if our love is rejected? What if our vulnerability is met with pain rather than acceptance? These haunting questions echo in the hearts of many, but they also provide a fertile ground for spiritual growth and introspection.

For the Seeker, the journey toward understanding extravagant love begins with a confrontation of societal expectations. In many cultures, love is often transactional; it demands conditions for its expression. We learn to love those who are similar, those who can reciprocate our feelings, and those who meet specific criteria for our affection. This conditional narrative weakens the true power of love. The Seeker struggles with these ideas, trying to understand how the teachings of the Gospel fit with what he observes in the world.

An essential pivot toward embracing extravagant love arises when the Seeker reflects on the radical examples of unconditional love present in the Bible. Consider Jesus's interactions with the marginalized and the sinners, the very individuals society deemed unworthy of love or redemption. His love did not come with stipulations; it was freely given, often surprising the recipients. The woman at the well, for instance, received acceptance and grace without pretense. Jesus's **extravagant love** reached beyond societal boundaries, illustrating that love can be transformative, especially when it is extended to those deemed undeserving.

As the Seeker delves into these narratives, he may find himself confronted with his own conditioning. This is where the struggle begins. There are layers of fear and hesitation to peel back, fear of rejection, of becoming vulnerable, of exposing oneself to potential hurt. These concerns often prevent individuals from fully pouring their love into others, especially those who appear different or unworthy. The Seeker's internal dialogue plays out like this: "What if my efforts are met with disdain?" or "What if I open my heart only to have it broken again?"

This inner conflict, though painful, serves as an invitation to deeper understanding. The Seeker comes to realize that loving extravagantly is not solely about the act of loving but also an internal journey toward self-acceptance and courage. As he wrestles with the definitions of love, he begins to see that love is not merely an emotion but a choice, a radical choice to join God in the act of loving even when it defies logic.

At this point, the Seeker's journey takes on a deeper layer. To embrace extravagant love, we must be willing to be vulnerable, to lower the walls that protect our hearts. Vulnerability isn't a sign of weakness; it shows the real strength that comes from love. It allows us to connect more deeply with others and mirrors God's love, which is full of generosity and acceptance. Such love reminds us that transformation often takes place in uncomfortable spaces, where we are challenged to move beyond fear into courage.

The concept of extravagant love invites us to see love not merely as a feeling but as a decision. Feelings are often fleeting, shaped by external circumstances or internal states. In contrast, the decision to love, especially when that love is countercultural and defies instinct, unlocks a transformative power within ourselves and in our relationships with others.

As the Seeker navigates this landscape, he begins to understand that true love operates in a realm beyond reason. It is radical precisely because it does not always adhere to societal expectations or practical considerations. It is a choice to move past the barriers of prejudice, fear, and disappointment. Here, the influence of God's extravagant love shines through, inviting the Seeker to cultivate a love that knows no bounds.

The account of Jesus washing His disciples' feet is a powerful illustration of servant-hearted love found in the New Testament. In addition to being radical, given the social customs of His day, this act of humility serves as a sobering reminder of the kind of love we are expected to exhibit. Jesus took the humble position of a servant, defying expectations and demonstrating that love is action-oriented, particularly towards those who might not reciprocate or appreciate it.

For the Seeker, this revelation leads to a deeper question: how can he embody this extravagant love within his own relationships? It is one thing to grasp the concept in theory, but the true challenge lies in its practice. He may pause to consider his daily interactions, how often does he extend himself toward those in need, even when it brings risk or discomfort? How often does he offer affection freely, without waiting for the assurance of love in return?

This journey calls the Seeker to adopt a mindset that recognizes the inherent worth of every person, an outlook that reflects God's own heart. He begins to see others not through the lens of flaws or shortcomings, but as worthy of love simply because they exist. This radical reframing of relationships invites him to embody a love that is both extravagant and transformative.

It is essential to explore the challenges and fears that accompany this radical choice of love. For many, including the Seeker, there is a deep-seated worry that loving extravagantly will lead to personal hurt or disappointment. Yet, in confronting these fears, he may discover that love's greatest rewards often emerge from moments of vulnerability.

When we allow ourselves to love without conditions or expectations, we uncover the profound joy that accompanies such selfless acts. This joy is often accompanied by a resilience that fortifies us against the inevitable trials of relationships. Rather than living in a realm of conditional love, the Seeker begins to understand that loving extravagantly can free him from the weight of always seeking to receive love in return.

Moreover, learning to practice extravagant love helps build a sense of community. The Seeker realizes that his actions can go beyond personal connections, inspiring others to live and love in the same way. When love operates from a place of abundance rather than scarcity, it inspires reciprocal acts that ripple throughout communities.

Community itself becomes a testament to the power of extravagant love. It thrives when individuals commit to embracing one another without fear or hesitation. This is evident in stories of individuals who step out of their comfort zones to care for those in need, whether through charitable acts, fostering relationships where love is needed, or simply offering a listening ear to those who feel isolated. The Seeker learns that fierce love does not require grand gestures; it often flourishes in the everyday moments that we choose to engage in, showing up for others in their joy, pain, and everything in between.

In the course of this examination of extravagant love, we also encounter the challenges that arise from societal norms. How does one navigate relationships in a world that often promotes self-preservation and self-interest? Discovering the path toward extravagant love may involve confronting the biases that shape our understanding of who is truly deserving of love. Whether rooted in race, socioeconomic status, or past mistakes, these biases demand deep reflection. The Seeker's inner journey toward love asks: *How do I love those whom society deems unworthy?*

For example, consider the story of the Prodigal Son, where the father's love remained steadfast despite his son's recklessness. This biblical narrative speaks powerfully about forgiveness and acceptance, a depiction of love that is consistently active, regardless of the circumstances. The Seeker, in his journey, begins to understand that love without hesitation echoes through stories like these, inviting him to extend the same grace to others he would wish for himself.

Through the exploration of extravagant love, the Seeker begins to form a personal definition of love that emphasizes vulnerability, generosity, and courage. This definition reflects an understanding that love's greatest power lies not in what it receives but in what it offers. In this light, the journey becomes less about seeking validation through love and more about becoming a beacon of love itself, illuminating the lives of others in need.

Ultimately, the essence of extravagant love culminates in a transformative freedom to love without limits, freely and without reservation. This understanding propels the Seeker into a life characterized by boldness and compassion, fueled by the realization that loving extravagantly is a reflection of God's Spirit within him. It is a rehearsal of the divine narrative, an ongoing invitation to share God's abundant love with a world yearning for acceptance and hope.

As he continues to reflect on the journey, the Seeker settles into the mantra that extravagant love, while challenging, is ultimately the most fulfilling pursuit he can undertake. He comes to understand that this kind of bold love isn't about having all the answers; it's about embracing the mystery of love that already exists within others. Every act of extravagant love becomes a powerful expression of faith, reminding him that love is meant to be shared and to grow.

In the end, understanding extravagant love shapes not only the Seeker's personal relationships but also redefines his interactions with the world at large. He realizes that although being vulnerable can lead to pain, it is also the path to genuine connection, a beautiful blend of love, grace, and unconditional acceptance. Through this lens, the Seeker embarks on a lifelong endeavor, committed to loving without reservation, ready to embrace the challenges, victories, and transformative power that come with such a mighty calling.

Vulnerability in Relationships

In the realm of love, we often find ourselves standing at a delicate intersection where vulnerability and connection meet. It is a crossroads that many fear to traverse, yet those who dare to journey down this path discover a depth of intimacy that is profoundly rewarding. To love extravagantly, as God intends, requires us to lay ourselves bare, to be open and honest about our fears, hopes, dreams, and, yes, even our wounds.

The concept of vulnerability is often misunderstood. Many see it as a weakness, a flaw that might expose them to hurt, ridicule, or judgment. However, what if we reframe vulnerability as the cornerstone of authentic relationships? As the Mentor often reminds the Seeker, "True love flourishes in the garden of vulnerability. It cannot grow in the sterile soil of defense mechanisms and emotional walls." This simple statement captures the core of what it means to be in relationships that are not only loving but also life changing.

As the Seeker pondered this idea, he reflected on his own life experiences, recalling moments when he felt a profound connection with another. Each memory was underscored by a willingness to share his true self, a decision to reveal his insecurities and dreams. He remembered one instance in particular, a conversation with a close friend that revealed the raw power of vulnerability.

It was one of those windy afternoons when they sat on a park bench with leaves fluttering around them. The Seeker had been feeling lost, navigating through a season of transition. As he spoke, his words came freely, each one mixed with emotions he had been holding back. He talked about his hopes for the future, but more importantly, he shared his fears, fears of failure, fears of isolation, and the overwhelming fear of never being enough. The friend listened intently, providing a safe space that felt both comforting and challenging.

In that moment, the Seeker chose to be vulnerable, choosing to risk the embarrassment of exposing the uncertainties. To his surprise, what followed was not judgment or pity, but a deep resonance. This friend shared his own struggles, revealing that he, too, had experienced such feelings. This openness transformed their relationship, laying a foundation of trust and understanding that was previously absent. In vulnerability, they found connection; in authenticity, they discovered love.

The Mentor often shared stories of individuals who had triumphed through vulnerability, illustrating the countless ways it can weave a thread of love and connection among people. One story that resonated deeply involved a woman named Trudy, who had struggled with the scars of a painful past. She had built walls around her heart, convinced that to be vulnerable would mean exposing herself to inevitable hurt. But one day, during a church gathering, Trudy felt a push, a gentle urging from within, beckoning her to share her story.

As she stood before her community, trembling yet resolute, she spoke of her battles, her triumphs, and the scars that seemed to define her. When she finished speaking, the room erupted in applause, but what surprised her most was the flurry of people who approached her afterward, individuals who thanked her for her bravery, people who shared their own stories of pain and healing. Through her vulnerability, Trudy created a safe space for others to express themselves; she ignited a sense of community built on mutual understanding.

The Seeker learned from Trudy's experience, realizing that vulnerability does not necessitate grand displays of emotion or exclusive stories of tragedy. Instead, it can be found in simple acts of openness, sharing a worry with a friend, admitting when one is struggling, or even expressing joy about personal achievements. However, the concept of exposing oneself can feel intimidating. It often leads to the question: What if I'm rejected? What if my vulnerability is met with indifference?

As the Mentor wisely advised, "The fear of rejection often keeps us caged in a prison of solitude. While rejection is indeed a possibility, it is imperative to remember that love, even in its wild and extravagant form, cannot exist without the risk of exposure. Each time you open your heart, you invite others to do the same."

This radical notion of love requires embracing the unpredictability that comes with genuine relationships. As the Seeker continued delving deeper into the subject, he recalled various interactions within his circle, family, friends, colleagues, and even acquaintances. He identified patterns of disconnect rooted in the unwillingness to engage with vulnerability. Conversations that scratched the surface but seldom penetrated the deeper layers of emotion.

The strength of love lies not in perfection but in imperfections shared. A perfect relationship might appear peaceful and pleasant, yet it lacks the heartbeat of authenticity. The most profound connections are characterized by shared struggles, laughter, and the collective journey toward understanding one another's hearts. The Seeker understood that to foster deeper bonds with others, he must first take the courageous step of embracing vulnerability himself.

A moving illustration of this idea occurred at a family get-together. The Seeker had frequently observed that family relationships were strained, as though everyone was hiding behind masks of detachment and civility. He impulsively chose to relate a personal story about a humiliating experience in his youth that had plagued him for years. As laughter filled the room, something shifted; a feeling of comfort and togetherness spread among them. Soon, others began sharing their own childhood mistakes, creating a rich and beautiful tapestry of shared memories. In that moment of vulnerability, the Seeker witnessed the walls melt away.

Emotionally rich relationships often spring from moments like these, where vulnerability serves as the glue, binding hearts together. However, choosing vulnerability doesn't come without risks. The Mentor, drawing from her own experiences, shared colorful narratives from her journey. She spoke of friendships shattered by perceived weakness, moments when being open had led to unintended consequences. Yet, as she reflected on these experiences, the overarching theme was that true relationships weather the storms born from vulnerability.

"I've learned," the Mentor said, "that while it's painful when vulnerability is met with a lack of compassion, the reward is far greater when you find those who reciprocate that openness. The right relationships will not only embrace your vulnerabilities; they will strengthen you through them. Every risk taken in love is a chance to connect at a deeper level."

This echo of wisdom resonated deeply within the Seeker. He began to recognize that his own reluctance to reveal his vulnerabilities often stemmed from a misguided fear of judgment. But as he took small steps toward openness, he found that others responded in kind. Each interaction was met with a mutual understanding, a beautiful give and take of emotional revelation that deepened the respect for one another.

Moreover, vulnerability is not just a gift we offer to others; it is also a gift we give ourselves. The Seeker realized that self-acceptance blossomed when he allowed himself to be vulnerable, shedding the layers of armor that had long protected him from perceived threats. By acknowledging his fears and insecurities, he began to explore them rather than hide them.

Throughout this inner journey, the Mentor encouraged continuous reflection. "Ask yourself," she suggested gently, "What areas of your life feel overly restrained? Where can you afford to be more open? Vulnerability isn't about becoming an open book; it's about sharing chapters that matter in your love story."

Armed with this newfound insight, the Seeker began to identify specific relationships in his life where he could practice vulnerability more freely. He sought opportunities to express feelings that had been left unspoken: gratitude toward a mentor, love for a partner, and understanding for a family member. Each open dialogue was a small act of courage, and with each step, he observed a clear shift, a deepening of connections that had long stayed superficial.

As this chapter of his life unfolded, the Seeker found himself cultivating relationships infused with authenticity. He discovered that with vulnerability came not just deeper connections but also the ability to connect with the vulnerability of others, a shared understanding of the human experience, and its myriad shades of joy and sorrow.

The Mentor often highlighted that in caring for others, we must not forget to care for ourselves as well. Vulnerability, although essential to forming connections, also requires self-compassion, the understanding that it is okay to feel fear, to falter, and to grow. "Be gentle with yourself," she advised. "Recognize that everyone navigates the complexities of vulnerability at their own pace. Your journey is unique to you, and that's where its beauty lies."

In the closing thoughts of this exploration, the Seeker no longer viewed vulnerability solely as a risk but as an adventure, an invitation to explore the boundless nature of love. He was reminded that each engagement with vulnerability was an opportunity not just to experience deeper connections but to witness the potential of true love.

As the Seeker looked back, he realized that every step taken down this path of vulnerability had been worth it. Each act of openness not only transformed his relationship with others but also created a more profound connection with himself. He discovered that when we dare to let go of our protective shells and accept the lovely chaos of being human, intimacy and closeness are born.

Vulnerability is a prominent and colorful thread in the vast fabric of love, connecting the experiences, hardships, and shared paths of countless individuals. As the Seeker reflected on his journey, he realized that this extravagant love we are invited into is not solely for the purpose of connection, but also for healing, growth, and ultimately for celebrating the exquisite fabric that love weaves among us all, imperfect in its embrace yet perfect in its intent.

Through the lens of vulnerability, he could now see love as an expansive force, one that not only draws him closer to others but also propels him toward an authentic relationship with himself. Ultimately, being vulnerable is an act of courage, an expression of love, not just for others, but also for one's own heart. It is in this delicate dance of openness that the true essence of love can flourish, extravagant and free.

Love that Transcends Boundaries

In a world filled with divisions, where labels often dictate boundaries between individuals, there lies an extraordinary depth of love capable of breaking through these barriers. This is the kind of love that rises above social, cultural, and situational limits, a love that goes against the usual logic of the world around us. As we set out on this exploration of extravagant love, we will examine moving stories, personal testimonies, and the transformational power of loving those who are outside of our comfort zones.

Consider the story of Luisa, who grew up in a tightly-knit community where tradition was valued highly. In her village, customs dictated whom one could love or befriend. The residents were cautious of outsiders, often viewing them through a lens clouded with suspicion and bias. However, when Luisa met Daniel, a young man from a neighboring town, everything changed. Daniel was different; he belonged to a different culture, spoke a different language, and practiced different beliefs. Yet, his heart throbbed with an unmistakable beat of love.

Luisa was at first hesitant, pulled between her upbringing and the magnetic connection she felt towards Daniel. She had been taught to fear and reject those from outside her community, but as she spent time with him, walls of prejudice began to crumble. She learned to appreciate the beautiful nuances of Daniel's culture, the stories of his ancestors, the songs of his people, and the flavors of his homeland. In their conversations, she discovered that love is a universal language that transcends any barrier that tries to contain it. It spreads like a warm breeze.

Gradually, Luisa's heart expanded in ways she had never imagined. She realized that the love she felt for Daniel was not just an infatuation but a gift that challenged her to embrace the richness of diversity. Together, they faced the disapproval of those around them. Friends turned cold, family members raised eyebrows, but the love that blossomed between them provided refuge and resilience. They became each other's safe haven, a fierce love that dared to defy the expectations laid upon them.

As we reflect on Luisa and Daniel's story, we must grapple with our own biases. Where do we draw the lines in our relationships? Are we willing to reach out, embrace, and love those who stand at the edges of our comfort zones? The Mentor reminds us that accepting and valuing diversity leads to deep personal growth, a kind of growth that mirrors God's boundless and generous love.

Next, let's explore the narrative of Amir, a refugee who fled his war-torn country in search of safety and hope. Arriving in a new land that felt foreign in every sense, Amir found himself grappling with loneliness, displacement, and fear. The local community welcomed him with mixed reactions: some offered open arms, while others turned away. It was during this tumultuous time that he met Elizabeth, a local resident who was deeply committed to service.

Elizabeth, undeterred by the differences that separated them, began to include Amir in community events, sharing meals and conversations that allowed their worlds to intertwine. She demonstrated that love is an action; it is found in the little moments when one reaches out past fear and bias. Through her kindness, Amir realized that love knows no borders or nationalities; it goes beyond the circumstances that often separate us.

Initially, Amir struggled to adjust. The memories of the past clung to him like shadows, whispering words of self-doubt and isolation. But with Elizabeth's unwavering support, he began to heal. Together, they explored each other's worlds, Elizabeth shared the stories of her ancestors, and Amir recounted tales of resilience and hope from his homeland. In their journey together, they broke down the walls of misunderstanding that separated them. Their friendship blossomed into a deep, abiding love strong enough to face societal scrutiny.

The love that Elizabeth exhibited for Amir is a profound testament to the extravagant love God exemplified: it unravels the threads of fear that hold us captive, inviting us to embrace others unconditionally. As we consider this relationship, we are encouraged to examine the connections in our lives: Are there people who stand on the outskirts, those we may overlook due to preconceived notions? The Mentor invites us to reach out, to open our hearts to the stories of others, and to allow their experiences to transform us.

As we turn to the narrative of Juan and Maria, two individuals from opposing ends of the socio-economic spectrum, we witness love's capability to break chains of inequality. Juan was born into privilege; his is a world where resources flowed freely, where opportunities were abundant. Maria, in stark contrast, came from a marginalized background, where each day was a battle for survival. In a society that often pitied or overlooked those like Maria, Juan found himself drawn to her strength and resilience.

Their love story was tense with challenges; both families disapproved, seeing only the chasms that separated them: wealth and poverty, privilege and struggle. Yet, Juan and Maria understood that love demands risk. They ventured into unfamiliar spaces, deepening their commitment to one another against the odds. With each encounter, they learned to see through each other's eyes, realizing that their love could bring about change, not just in their lives, but in the lives of others.

In reflecting on their journey, we recognize that loving **extravagantly** requires us to confront systemic barriers. How can we advocate for love in environments that favor exclusivity? The Mentor guides us in this understanding, emphasizing the power of context and encouraging us to challenge structures that assign worth to individuals based on their circumstances.

Each story we've explored demonstrates the transformative power of love that defies boundaries. This **extravagance**, the willingness to accept those who are different, is deeply rooted in Jesus' teachings. He spent time with tax collectors and sinners, reaching out to those rejected by society. He sat with tax collectors and sinners, engaging those ostracized by society. His love was radical, shattering expectations and inviting others into the fold. As we engage with these narratives, we must ask ourselves: *How do we embody such love?*

The Seeker wrestles with these questions, considering what it means to navigate friendships, relationships, and communities filled with disparities. The Mentor gently nudges, reminding the Seeker that to embody God's love means extending hands of friendship to those who remain untouched. We can rethink our interactions by inviting the unknown and unexpected into our circles by adopting this expectation perspective.

Take a moment to visualize the faces of those around you: coworkers, classmates, neighbors. Who might you be overlooking? The Mentor encourages us to see beyond superficial connections, to take risks in love by engaging with those who differ, whether in background, beliefs, or experiences. In doing so, we not only expand our understanding of others but also deepen our connections, allowing love to transcend the labels we so often cling to.

Now, let's reflect on the story of Linda, a woman whose heart was set aflame by her work with the less fortunate in her community. She approached those whom many others avoided, seeing beyond their circumstances to the humanity within. Linda learned that each person had a unique story, an intricate tapestry woven through hardship and dreams. One day, she met a man named Kevin, who had fought a long battle with addiction and abandonment. While others saw him as just a statistic, Linda saw the person behind the struggles.

Over time, Linda cultivated a relationship with Kevin, providing support and companionship as he navigated the tumultuous waters of recovery. Their relationship showed what extravagant love truly looks like, a love unafraid of vulnerability and one that saw Kevin's worth beyond his current struggles. Through Linda's devotion, Kevin experienced love's power to heal and was able to take back his own story.

As we consider Linda's testimony, we are invited to reflect on how we can integrate such actions into our own lives. Love, after all, often reveals itself through simple yet profound gestures. The Mentor encourages us to find beauty in small acts, the warm smile shared with a stranger, the words of affirmation offered to a colleague, the support extended to someone grappling with their identity. Such actions ripple outward, instigating transformation in ways we may never fully comprehend.

The narratives we've explored highlight the vast landscape of human connection painted by the strokes of extravagant love. They reinforce the understanding that love does not exist in a vacuum; it is a dynamic force capable of inspiring hope and healing. The Mentor's voice echoes in our hearts, urging us onward: to engage, to listen, to love without reservation.

As the Seeker contemplates these lessons, he is reminded of God's infinite grace, a grace that beckons us to love one another as He loves us. Each story invites us to walk alongside our fellow human beings, inviting the marginalized and the forgotten into our lives.

We conclude this subchapter with a call to action. To love extravagantly is to embrace the beauty of our shared humanity. It is to learn from the relationships we cultivate, to nurture acceptance, and to foster understanding. Let us become conduits of this love, navigating the complexities of our diverse world with compassion and openness, a reflection of God's overwhelming, transformative love.

As we step into the world, let us remember that love knows no boundaries. It invites us to break down the walls that divide, to seek out the lost, and to embrace the diversity that colors our existence. In this journey of extravagant love, may we find our hearts expanded, our lives enriched, and our understanding deepened, as we learn to embody God's love in all its glorious forms.

Chapter 4:
Receiving Love

Barriers to Accepting Love

Many of us find ourselves in a complicated dance with the idea of being loved, especially by God, in a world that teems with the joy of love but is obscured by numerous obstacles. When we talk of divine love, we frequently picture its unadulterated, transformational nature—a love that is unconditional and unfailing. However, when confronted with how immense God's love really is, we may unknowingly put up walls that stop us from fully accepting it. Even though we claim to want love and seek it in various ways, hidden fears or doubts can hinder our ability to connect with others and receive the love we deeply yearn for. Self-doubt emerges as one of the most insidious barriers to accepting love. It whispers continually, reminding us of our shortcomings and failures, casting shadows over our inherent worthiness. It asks, "How could you possibly be deserving of love, particularly divine love?" This nagging voice often takes root in our past experiences — childhood wounds, relationships that left us feeling unworthy, and insecurities that societal standards have reinforced. We begin to internalize these messages until they become part of who we are. As the old saying goes, 'what we dwell on, we become.' When we think of ourselves as unlovable, we begin to act as if we are intrinsically unworthy of love, feeding the cycle of doubt and fear.

We may encounter situations that make us feel rejected or despised, or instances that seem to confirm our anxieties as we navigate the path of self-doubt. Maybe it was a buddy who abandoned you when you needed them most, or a parent who found it difficult to show affection. These experiences can leave emotional scars that influence how we see the world. They might make us question God's plans or wonder if we've done something wrong that makes us unworthy of His constant love. When we look at God's love through the lens of our own doubts and limits, it can seem confusing, even though deep down we know His love has no limits and covers everything.

The challenge lies in breaking down these barriers. It requires courage and a willingness to confront those inner voices echoing our worthlessness. It would be beneficial to explore the scriptures, which continuously invite us into a loving relationship with the divine. In 1 John 4:19, we are reminded, "We love because He first loved us." This profound truth should speak loudly over the whispers of self-doubt, changing our narrative from unworthiness to acceptance. Allowing ourselves to recognize our inherent value as children of God becomes the first step towards dismantling this barrier.

Past trauma also plays a significant role in shaping our relationship with love. The things we've been through can make us feel like we don't deserve love and make it hard for us to open our hearts to others. Trauma doesn't always come from big events, it can also come from small but powerful moments when love was only given under certain conditions or taken away without warning. Such events may carry pain, disappointment, or betrayal, causing us to associate love with hurt rather than healing. The heart that has known pain often builds resilience by developing protective mechanisms, but these same mechanisms can hinder our ability to fully receive love when it is offered.

In recognizing this barrier, we must approach our trauma with compassion. Acknowledge that our past does not define our future, nor does it dictate our eligibility to receive God's love. As we reflect on our experiences, we can take some time to unpack how these past hurts affect our current relationships, not only with God but also with family, friends, and even ourselves. Forgiveness, both to ourselves and those who have hurt us, can become a liberating force, allowing love to flow more freely through our lives. The process may look different for each individual, but faith plays a vital role in undertaking this deeply introspective journey.

Another difficult obstacle to accepting love is societal expectations. We are frequently burdened by irrational expectations in a world filled with cultural messages about what love should look like. Society often gives us a false idea of what real love looks like, whether it's the fairy tale endings we heard as kids or the picture-perfect relationships we see on Instagram. These messages can make us feel like we're not good enough, like we have to be perfect to be loved or feel worthy before we can truly love others.

This pervasive influence can lead to feelings of inadequacy. We may believe that we must follow certain prescriptions to be worthy of love, reinforcing the barriers we already have. However, the Gospel reveals a different story — one where love does not come with conditions or expectations. Love, especially divine love, is radical and transformative, breaking through the confines of societal norms. Jesus' love challenges our ideals; it does not wait for us to become perfect. Rather, it meets us where we are, in our authenticity and flaws, inviting us into a space of acceptance and grace.

To dismantle the barriers formed by societal expectations, we need to recalibrate our understanding of love. Reflecting on the nature of Christ's love can furnish us with clarity—love does not operate on a ledger. It does not tally up our flaws or reserve affection for those who fit a particular mold. The story of the Prodigal Son illustrates this beautifully. The father's unconditional love persisted even when the son had squandered his inheritance, illustrating that love's grace is available to all, irrespective of our human missteps.

In exploring our barriers to accepting love, it is essential to engage in self-reflection and take inventory of the messages we have received about love throughout our lives. We must ask ourselves: What do we believe about love? Where did these beliefs come from? By unpacking our narratives, we can begin to identify and deconstruct harmful beliefs about our worthiness to receive love.

A significant part of this introspection involves understanding that the fear of vulnerability often compounds our fears. Vulnerability, in essence, is the root of all genuine connection. Yet, it is a daunting task to allow ourselves to be seen fully and completely, especially when we harbor doubts and fears concerning our worthiness. The fear of rejection lingers in the background, narrating stories of past wounds that hold the power to deter us from opening ourselves up to love.

For many, the act of stepping into vulnerability feels like stepping into an abyss. "What if they don't love me back?" "What if they see my flaws and decide I'm not worth it?" But in this space of vulnerability lies the unique opportunity for authentic love to flourish. It is precisely in our openness that we often discover a greater love, one that reflects God's acceptance despite our imperfections.

To truly be open and vulnerable, we need to grow closer to God, who welcomes us into His complete and unconditional love. The Psalms remind us to give our worries to Him and be open to His comfort. When we come to God with our struggles, we learn that His love doesn't come with conditions; He doesn't require us to be perfect to feel close to Him. Acknowledging our need for love, without fear of judgment, allows us to explore unfathomable depths of acceptance.

As we become aware of the barriers that stifle our acceptance of love, we also realize that these obstacles can be dismantled through community. Engaging with others who share a faith-centered perspective allows us to nurture an environment where love is openly discussed and experienced. In the fellowship of believers, we can share our stories, our fears, and our barriers, finding solidarity and strength in the collective journey.

Imagine a space where vulnerability is tenderly supported, where traumas are gently shared, and where self-doubt is met with reassurance and encouragement. In such an environment, genuine love flourishes. The Spirit thrives in community, fostering connections that bring to light the often-invisible barriers we carry. Embracing one another in love creates a safe haven where the barren landscapes of our hearts can be nurtured again.

Ultimately, our barriers to accepting love hinge not only on self-doubt and societal expectations but also on the misconceptions we hold about the divine nature of love itself. We are drawn to God because He first loved us, yet we often distort that love through the lens of our experiences, fears, and societal teachings.

To accept God's love is to recognize that His affection extends beyond the individual and into the community. Connecting with others who are also on this journey of understanding divine love can provide encouragement and support as we face our barriers together. By witnessing the struggles and triumphs of others, we glean insights into our own challenges, fostering a culture of love and acceptance.

As we continue on this journey towards embracing the fullness of God's love, we must be patient with ourselves. Acceptance takes time and involves facing some uncomfortable truths about ourselves. Our barriers won't dissipate overnight, but with introspection, prayer, and community, we can work through our hesitations and fears. We can begin to dismantle the self-imposed limitations that have defined our understanding of love for far too long.

Let us remember that God's love is an ocean that welcomes us as we are, without demands or expectations. Even when we feel unworthy, His love remains steadfast, never contingent upon our performance. In our most vulnerable moments, we are invited to cast aside our fear and to embrace the incredible truth that we are inherently worthy of love, exactly as we are.

When we face and work through the things that hold us back, we get closer to God, to ourselves, and to the people around us. This helps love, both God's love and love from others, flow more freely in our lives. As a result, we can enjoy the deep, full life of love that God always wanted for us. The process may be challenging, but with each step we take, we move closer to a reality where love can be freely given and received, transforming our hearts and lives into reflections of the overwhelming, never-ending, boundless love of God.

Opening Our Hearts

Opening our hearts to love can feel scary, like standing on the edge of a cliff, caught between fear and trust. It takes courage to be vulnerable and let others see our true selves. But when we do, we open ourselves to something powerful - God's deep, unconditional love. Yet, in a world where conditions and expectations frequently surround love, this act can seem difficult, if not impossible.

Learning to open our hearts takes effort and the bravery to step outside of what feels safe or familiar. As we explore the importance of being open in our spiritual lives, we can discover helpful steps and spiritual habits that make it easier to welcome God's love into our hearts. The Mentor, wise and patient, shares a personal encounter that marked the beginning of her own journey towards openness. "I still remember standing in the dim light of my room, trembling with isolation and fear. I had built walls around my heart—walls that were both a shield and a prison. One night, feeling utterly alone, I prayed for the first time in years, asking God to help me open my heart to Him."

This prayer was a pivotal moment in the Mentor's life. It served as a catalyst, igniting a desire to learn how to embrace the love she had long felt unworthy to receive. It marked the beginning of a beautiful journey, characterized by openness, vulnerability, and acceptance of the divine affection that pursued her relentlessly.

To follow in the Mentor's footsteps, we must first understand the barriers that make receiving love challenging. Often, these barriers manifest as self-doubt, past hurts, or preconceived notions about the conditions of love. Humanly, we may find ourselves grappling with guilt over past mistakes or keeping others at arm's length due to a fear of rejection. Acknowledging these barriers is an important first step toward healing.

Reflective Exercise: Take a moment to contemplate your own barriers to receiving love. What fears arise when you think about opening your heart? Write them down, and confront them.

For many, including the Mentor, the journey of opening one's heart involves practicing self-compassion. Understanding that we are all imperfect vessels, striving to learn and grow, invites us to extend grace not only to ourselves but also to others. "There was a time when I struggled with guilt stemming from poor decisions," the Mentor recalls. "I had to learn that God's love does not hinge on my performance or my failures. In fact, it was precisely my imperfections that drew me closer to His heart."

As we learn to practice self-compassion, we can begin to cultivate the habit of acceptance. How do we accept love? By creating mental and emotional spaces that welcome it. This is not merely about thinking positively; rather, it involves intentionally creating an environment within ourselves where love can reside. This process encourages us to let go of preconceived notions about who deserves love and who doesn't.

Practical Step: Set aside a few moments each day for quiet contemplation. Close your eyes, breathe deeply, and visualize your heart opening like a flower under the warmth of the sun. Imagine God's love pouring in, nourishing you, and filling you with peace. Allow yourself to feel this acceptance, if only for a brief moment.

The Mentor introduces the concept of vulnerability in this journey toward openness. "Vulnerability was a foreign concept to me," she admits, "Yet I discovered it was a vital component of connecting with God and others." Vulnerability requires us to share our authentic selves, to open up about our journeys, our struggles, and our dreams. It may feel risky, but it also fosters deeper connections and a greater sense of belonging.

Reflective Exercise: Write about a moment when you allowed yourself to be vulnerable, either with God or someone you trust. What was the experience like? What feelings arose during and after this moment?

As we learn to be more open and vulnerable, spiritual practices can help us maintain an open heart. One powerful habit is prayer, talking honestly with God about our hopes, fears, and dreams. The Mentor reminds us that it's important to let go and fully trust God during these moments of prayer. "One evening, during a particularly lonely season, I prayed not for answers but for the ability to surrender my heart to God. In that moment of surrender, I felt a profound peace settle over me."

Incorporating prayer into our daily routines can deepen our relationship with God, rejuvenating our desire to receive love. Each morning, consider dedicating your first moments to God through prayer. Present your heart, your fears, and your openness, inviting God to fill it with love.

Another powerful spiritual practice is the act of gratitude. Expressing gratitude opens our hearts to recognize the abundance of love present in our lives. Daily, we can cultivate a mind and heart attuned to the love we have received, both from God and from those around us.

Practical Step: Start a gratitude journal, listing three things each day that you are grateful for. Allow this practice to remind you of the many ways love finds its way into your life.

It is also essential to examine the influence of external relationships on our ability to open our hearts. The Mentor reflects on the journey to surround herself with individuals who demonstrated love and support, emphasizing how important these connections were in the healing process. "I sought out friendships that nurtured my spirit, which encouraged me to embrace vulnerability and express my heart freely."

Community plays a critical role in our journey toward love. Being part of a supportive network fosters an environment that encourages acceptance and celebrates our uniqueness. This community can be found within a church, a support group, or simply a circle of friends who uplift one another.

Reflective Exercise: Consider your current relationships. Who in your life embodies the love and acceptance you wish to receive? How can you deepen your connections with these individuals?

As we continue to learn how to open our hearts, it's essential to take time to reflect on ourselves regularly. When we understand our own emotions, we can see where we might be closed off. The mentor suggests spending quiet time alone to help us listen to our thoughts and feelings more clearly. "In stillness, I often discovered layers of hurt and pain that had been buried," she stated. "Acknowledging these emotions was the first step to releasing them."

Taking time to be still, whether through meditation, nature walks, or quiet contemplation, affords us the opportunity to process our emotions and draw closer to God. Engaging in reflective journaling can also help clear mental clutter and create clarity around our feelings.

Practical Step: Dedicate specific times during your week for solitude. Use these moments to meditate, pray, or reflect on your emotional state. What thoughts or feelings arise in these times of stillness?

As our hearts begin to open, we may discover the joy that comes from embracing God's love. It is a profound experience, one that transcends our understanding and fills our beings with light. The Mentor shares, "When I began to receive God's love, the weight of my past started to dissolve. I realized that I am infinitely cherished, just as I am."

This realization is powerful; it brings a deep sense of inner peace, reassuring us that we are never alone. As the walls surrounding our hearts weaken, we discover a new openness not just to divine love but to self-love and love for others.

Reflective Exercise: Spend a moment writing about how it feels to imagine receiving God's love without limitations. What does this love look like? How does it transform your perception of yourself and your life?

The process of opening our hearts does not happen overnight. It is a gradual process, requiring patience and tenderness towards ourselves. As we learn to accept God's love, we also learn to extend that love outward, transforming our relationships and the communities in which we live.

In closing, it is essential to remember that the act of receiving love is also about joy—the joyful acceptance of who we are and who we are loved to be. As we become more attuned to God's love, we find ourselves filled with gratitude and an abundance of peace, which then radiates into every aspect of our lives.

The Mentor concludes, "Embracing God's timeless love transformed me from the inside out. I began to see love everywhere—within me, in others, and in the world around me. This transformation brought immeasurable joy and a desire to share that love with everyone. It is a journey worth embarking on, a reality awaiting all who dare to open their hearts."

Let's go on this journey together, learning to make room in our hearts to receive God's endless and unconditional love fully. As we do, our own lives become richer, and we become a source of love and kindness to others; that's something truly special. So, open your heart, dear reader, and let love in.

Community Support in Acceptance

In our journey toward understanding and accepting love, community plays an essential role. Love is not merely a personal experience; it thrives in the context of relationships and shared experiences. As we navigate the complexities of accepting God's love and loving ourselves, the importance of community cannot be overstated. It becomes a pillar that supports and nurtures our growth, guiding us through the struggles and triumphs of our emotional and spiritual lives.

Throughout history, communities have served as sources of connection, encouragement, and understanding. The Bible frequently emphasizes the importance of fellowship among believers, illustrating how individuals encourage and support one another in their faith journeys. In Acts 2:44-47, we see a beautiful description of the early church, where believers shared everything in common, worshiped together, and provided for each other's needs. This vibrant community was not just a gathering of people; it was a living testament to the love of God in action. They demonstrated how embracing love and acceptance could create an environment rich in support and nurturing, allowing everyone to flourish.

Yet, the challenge lies in recognizing and actively participating in such communities. For many, the idea of reaching out for help can feel discouraging. Past experiences of rejection or disappointment may create barriers that inhibit us from fully engaging with others. Some may feel unworthy of support or believe their struggles are too burdensome for others. However, it is vital to understand that community is not a space where perfection is required; rather, it is a sanctuary for imperfection, a gathering of those seeking love, understanding, and connection.

To begin fostering an environment of acceptance, we must first learn to identify the supportive relationships in our lives. Sometimes we don't notice the people already in our lives who are ready to support us. These can be friends, family, coworkers, or members of our church or community. To find these caring people, we can start by thinking about who around us shows love and acceptance. Who in our lives demonstrates unconditional love? Who has shown compassion when we've felt lost or unworthy? These individuals can become the anchors in our journey toward accepting love.

Once we've identified our support network, the next essential step is to initiate contact. Vulnerability is a fundamental aspect of accepting love, and it often requires us to step out of our comfort zones. This can be accomplished by reaching out to someone we trust and sharing our thoughts and feelings. We might say, "I've been struggling with accepting love, and I would love your insight." This openness can foster deeper conversations, allowing the relationship to blossom. Remember, the act of seeking support is not a sign of weakness; it is a courageous step toward healing and acceptance.

As we cultivate these supportive relationships, it is equally important to reciprocate the love and support we receive. Community is a two-way street, and actively engaging in relationships fosters a sense of belonging and trust. This reciprocal dynamic reinforces the community's foundation, creating a safe space where all members feel valued and appreciated. When we listen to others, offer a helping hand, or share in their burdens, we help create an atmosphere that nurtures the growth of love.

Moreover, community support thrives on shared experiences. When we gather together, whether in small group settings or larger gatherings, we contribute to a collective understanding of love. These moments reveal that love can manifest in various ways, through laughter, shared hardships, or simply being present in silence. When we share our stories of struggles and victories, we encourage others and remind them they're not alone on their journey. In turn, hearing the stories of others can illuminate our paths, revealing how God's love can shine through the experiences of those around us.

We are often prompted to reach out to others when we hear their struggles. Our natural inclination to extend compassion reflects the love of God within us. In Galatians 6:2, we are reminded, "Carry each other's burdens, and in this way, you will fulfill the law of Christ." This call to support one another is the very essence of community. Embracing this philosophy in our interactions not only aids others but also fosters our growth in love.

It is also essential to seek out communities that align with our desire for acceptance and love. Transitioning into a new community can be intimidating, but finding groups that prioritize growth and understanding can significantly influence our journey. This might involve joining a church group, signing up for community outreach programs, or participating in support groups. Engaging with individuals who also value love and acceptance can significantly diminish feelings of isolation or insecurity.

As we create and participate in love-filled spaces, we must consistently practice openness and vulnerability. It is through this shared commitment to authenticity that meaningful connections can flourish. Whether in a small group Bible study or a broader church gathering, approaching these interactions with a willingness to be open can inspire others to do the same. As we share our fears, joys, and experiences, we build bridges of understanding and empathy that enable love to thrive.

While seeking community support is vital, it is important to acknowledge that communities are not without their challenges. Misunderstandings, differences in opinions, and conflicts may arise. However, navigating these challenges can provide invaluable lessons about love and acceptance. Each difficulty offers an opportunity to engage in constructive dialogue, fostering growth for both ourselves and our communities. In these instances, the key is to practice patience and compassion. When faced with conflict, we are encouraged to breathe, listen, and approach conversations with an open heart, ready to understand perspectives that may differ from our own.

It is also crucial to acknowledge the importance of addressing and discussing barriers within communities. Talking about tough topics like mental health, trauma, and acceptance can help break the shame and silence around them. When we speak openly, we create a safe space where people feel comfortable sharing their struggles. These honest conversations help build more loving and accepting communities. Moreover, community members can serve as reminders of God's ever-present love. When we gather, we have the opportunity to witness God's love in action through one another. As we share scripture, pray together, or simply engage in fellowship, we create an atmosphere where God's love can be felt and celebrated. These moments provide a strong foundation upon which our understanding of love deepens.

As we connect with supportive communities, it's important to remember the significance of gratitude. Showing appreciation, whether with a thank-you note or just a kind word, helps strengthen our relationships and brings people closer together. Gratitude not only uplifts those we are thankful for but also reinforces our commitment to creating a loving environment. This simple act can go a long way in fostering emotional connections rooted in appreciation and recognition.

Additionally, involvement in community service can beautifully exemplify love in action. Sharing love through acts of service cultivates a profound sense of connection among members. Organizing a community event, volunteering at a local charity, or participating in outreach activities allows individuals to come together, united by a common cause. It not only serves as an expression of love but also reminds us that in loving others, we experience the love of God in deeper ways.

As we reflect on the importance of community in the journey of accepting love, let us remember to nurture and celebrate the relationships that enrich our lives. They can become the champions who guide us through our struggles, reminding us that we are worthy of love and affection. Each interaction, each shared experience, can draw us closer to understanding God's unconditional love, allowing us to mirror that love in our actions and connections.

Taking the time to cultivate supportive relationships is an essential step. Embracing the teachings of love creates an environment where acceptance can flourish. As we venture forth, let us not only seek support but also be supporters of one another, recognizing that love finds its fullest expression in community. By investing in these connections, we can foster communities ripe for love, acceptance, and profound transformation.

In closing, we are called to create and engage in environments that celebrate love and acceptance. It is through shared experiences, supportive relationships, and acts of service that we become living embodiments of God's love in action. The journey isn't always easy, but when we build and participate in communities filled with love, we begin to understand what it truly means to accept love. Let's be encouraged to show up in our communities with open hearts, willing to both give and receive love, and through that, our lives and the lives of others can be changed for the better. In this beautiful cycle of giving and receiving, love blossoms into something even greater than we could have imagined—one heart at a time.

Chapter 5:
Reflecting His Love

Embodiment of Love

The world often feels like a chaotic and overwhelming place, where love seems contingent on circumstances and appearances. Yet, in the middle of confusion and uncertainty, there's still a quiet invitation, an invitation to live with love in everything we do, think, and say. For those who seek to live in alignment with God's love, the path is both straightforward and deeply meaningful. It's about showing love through even the smallest actions. This way of living can change not just our own lives, but also the lives of others around us, spreading kindness far and wide.

Our Seeker, walking through this labyrinth of life, guides us through his experiences of striving to reflect God's love. His encounters illuminate the truth that small acts of love can have a monumental impact. The journey is riddled with challenges, misunderstandings, and moments of doubt; yet, within these struggles lie opportunities for growth, understanding, and the reaffirmation of God's love, as it is manifested in everyday life.

When we take on the role of a Seeker, we begin to notice and think about the small but meaningful acts of kindness that are often overlooked. Perhaps it begins in a bustling restaurant. Instead of rushing through the line with impatience, the Seeker chooses to pause and offer a smile or a kind word to the servers, recognizing that their day may be filled with unseen burdens. This small act, this simple gesture, makes a big difference. It reminds the servers that they matter, something they might forget in the busy routine of their day. In that moment, the Seeker becomes a channel for God's love, showing care and kindness.

The Seeker shares how he has made a conscious effort to practice kindness daily. Each encounter with someone becomes an opportunity for love to flow through them. A small act, such as saying "thank you," smiling warmly, or holding the door for someone, can have a significant impact. The Seeker thinks about times when someone's heartfelt thanks seemed to lighten the whole mood, reminding him how deeply connected we all are.

The love he chooses to show inspires others too, encouraging him to keep spreading kindness in his own life.

As we trace the Seeker's experiences, he begins to understand that embodying love isn't limited to moments of serenity or clarity. Instead, it reveals itself amid frustrations and difficulties. During a particularly tense day at work, when tempers run high, how does the Seeker respond? In this scenario, love requires him to pause, breathe, and respond rather than react. Consciously choosing to approach grumpy colleagues with empathy provides an opportunity to defuse tension with kindness and compassion. "How can I assist you?" or "I understand this is difficult; let's find a solution together," becomes his mantra. In these moments, it's easy to see how embodying love requires intentionality. It isn't about perfection, but authenticity; it's about meeting people where they are with open hearts.

The Seeker confronts challenges with this simple philosophy: to reflect God's love means to embrace vulnerability, especially when faced with opposition or misunderstanding. Some days, he will falter. There are moments when frustration takes over, and love feels distant. The Seeker grapples with these realities, recognizing that embodying love is not a destination but a journey—a dance between aspiration and the humanness of existence.

One striking encounter illustrates this perfectly. The Seeker finds himself face-to-face with an elderly neighbor who often seems withdrawn. The neighbor's home is overgrown with weeds, and the yard looks neglected. With little hesitation, the Seeker makes a decision: he will spend an afternoon helping to tidy up the garden. It's a small undertaking, but the impact feels monumental. As they work side by side, conversation flows, revealing layers of loneliness and stories untold. The neighbor's laughter reveals a melody of gratitude, a reminder of the healing power of love in action.

As the Seeker reflects on this experience, he comes to recognize the lesson that love is often found in the spaces where we step outside of our comfort zones. These actions might not lead to big or immediate results, and they may not always bring the reaction we hope for, but what matters is that we show up and try. Life unfolds moment by moment, and each act of love, no matter how small, has the power to brighten someone's day and make a meaningful difference.

Yet, we cannot ignore the doubts that arise in the Seeker's heart. Are his efforts enough? Do small acts even make a difference? This inner dialogue prompts him to remember that love doesn't measure itself by worldly standards or expectations. Instead, it resides in the intention behind every action. The Seeker recalls the story of the Widow's Mite from the Gospels, where Jesus commends a woman for giving a small coin, more than the wealthy who gave out of abundance. This alludes to the truth that love's worth is not in its magnitude but in its authenticity. The Seeker realizes that tears, even in the smallest of choices, can carry the weight of God's love when shared sincerely.

The journey does not solely reflect upon the Seeker's experiences; it invites readers to engage in their own reflections. Where can love find a home in the everyday? Where can they sow seeds of kindness? It might be as simple as calling a friend who's been on their mind or writing a thank you note to someone who has made a difference in their life. The Seeker's narrative encourages readers to find their own expressions of love, to discover just how rich their lives become when they consciously decide to embody God's love.

In moments of reflection, the Seeker understands that there will be seasons of both drought and abundance. Embodying God's love isn't about a constant flow; it's about recognizing the rhythms of life and showing up even when the well feels dry. During those harder times, the Seeker reminds himself to be gentle with his own heart. Love is not just something he gives but also something he must allow himself to receive. The act of giving may feel rewarding, but the act of receiving is equally vital; it fosters a nurturing cycle through which love flows freely.

So, the Seeker decides to build relationships that nurture love. Being part of a community that values love helps him feel truly connected. Together, they support and inspire one another to show God's love in their daily lives, creating a circle of kindness. The realization begins to take root: the more they give, the more they cultivate space for receiving love, which only fuels further acts of generosity.

The Seeker learns that embodying love is a reflection of a divine truth—that love begets love. It permeates every interaction, causing enormous reverberations in a world that frequently seems divided. He realizes that even when he's hurt or misunderstood, he can still choose to respond with love. By doing this, he can turn negative situations into moments of kindness and healing. Thinking about this, he feels moved to take action, to mend broken relationships and show love even to those he once misunderstood.

This leads to the contemplation of forgiveness, interwoven with the embodiment of love. The Seeker recognizes that to live out love is, at times, to forgive the unforgivable. It is to extend compassion to those who wrong us, much like how God extends grace towards us. In these moments of struggle, the Seeker reflects on the act of forgiveness as a choice, a choice to embody God's love even when it feels difficult.

Toward the chapter's end, the Seeker invites readers to view every encounter as an opportunity. What if, in every moment, we approached situations asking, "How can I embody love here?" What if our reflections challenged us to be the first to extend grace, to initiate kindness, or to embrace vulnerability? The Seeker inspires us with a poignant understanding: while we each possess different strengths, we can embody love by being ourselves—authentic, open, and willing.

The challenge of embodiment becomes clear: it exists in our choices, our responses, and our willingness to see the divine in each person we meet. No act of love is too small; every kind gesture helps bring people together through God's love. When we choose to live with love, we find meaning not just in our own lives but also in the bigger story of connection and belonging. Each choice to act with kindness shapes the reality we share, drawing others into a deeper experience of love.

Thus, we conclude this exploration of embodiment with a heartfelt question: How shall we choose to embody love today? The pathway to reflecting God's love is a beautiful journey, one that begins with a single step into the realm of compassionate action, inviting others along the way. May we strive not merely to love but to embody love, letting it shape our lives and those around us through the simple yet heartfelt power of divine affection.

Love in Diverse Contexts

Love isn't limited to a singular expression; it flourishes in many parts of our lives. This deep and powerful feeling looks different in families, friendships, workplaces, and communities, but it's just as important in each one. Each context provides a unique lens through which we can examine the transformative power of love. It invites us to explore not only how we give and receive love in these settings but also the challenges and rewards that accompany our relationships.

Love is the foundation of every family. It's the caring force that holds parents, children, siblings, and relatives together. Families often provide the first experiences of love, instilling values and shaping our understanding of relationships. However, navigating familial love can be complicated, particularly when misunderstandings arise or conflicts emerge. Sibling rivalry, generational gaps, and differing opinions can create tension, challenging the essence of familial love.

Imagine a household where siblings cannot seem to get along. Ruth and Emily, two sisters, often find themselves bickering over trivial matters, which leads to growing resentment. Their parents, distressed by the ongoing disputes, decide to intervene. They organize family meetings where each family member can express their feelings without interruption. In these sessions, Ruth and Emily begin to understand the motivations behind each other's actions, allowing them to bridge the gap that has been created.

Through these shared dialogues, the sisters rediscover their bond and nurture a deeper understanding of love that transcends conflict. They learn the importance of empathy, patience, and forgiveness within their familial dynamic. In this way, love becomes a transforming force, capable of resolving disputes and fostering unity.

Similarly, friendships also have the power to deeply affect our lives through love. They give us a safe space to be ourselves, share our feelings, and support each other. This kind of love is often marked by loyalty and true companionship. However, this relationship is not without its challenges. Friends may drift apart due to life changes, misunderstandings, or unexpressed needs.

Take the example of Steve and Jake, who have been friends since childhood. As they grew older, their paths diverged. Steve pursued a career in finance while Jake became a teacher. Their different lifestyles led to a growing distance, and soon, an unspoken tension developed between them. Rather than allowing their friendship to fade, Steve reaches out to Jake, suggesting a monthly catch-up. They agree to plan outings that allow them to reconnect, sharing their struggles and joys.

Through this commitment to maintaining their friendship, they discover that love within this context is about intentionality. They learn that friendships require effort and effective communication, especially during times of transition. As they dedicate time to nurture their bond, they find themselves reinvigorated, realizing that true friendship adapts to life's changes—even the mundane moments can become extraordinary through shared experiences.

Moving beyond family and friendships, workplaces can embody a culture of love that fosters productivity and well-being. Work environments, though often perceived as transactional, are increasingly recognized as communities where relationships matter. The dynamics of workplace love can significantly affect job satisfaction and overall morale. When companies embrace a culture of love—through respect and supportive interactions—employees feel valued and engaged.

Consider a company that has recently undergone significant restructuring. Employees, feeling uncertain and anxious, are hesitant to engage with their colleagues. Recognizing this tension, the management implements team-building exercises and wellness initiatives that encourage connection. By creating safe spaces for dialogue, employees can share their concerns and aspirations.

Through this initiative, a culture of love begins to flourish. Colleagues form bonds, champion each other's successes, and provide support during setbacks. In this context, love shows up as teamwork and support. It goes beyond just getting along; it builds trust and cooperation. When employees feel this kind of connection, they're more motivated to work together toward a shared goal, and it helps create a positive and united workplace.

Communities too, are held together by everyday acts and expressions of love. A vibrant community thrives on the relationships among its members and the ways they engage with one another. Community love goes beyond surface interactions; it thrives on mutual respect, shared values, and collective goals. However, love in communities can also be challenged by division and conflict, particularly in diverse neighborhoods where differences are more noticeable.

Consider a neighborhood dealing with a contentious issue, like zoning for a new development. The residents' views differ according to how the suggested changes will affect their daily lives. As disputes arise between groups, each arguing for their own viewpoint, tension builds. However, people are encouraged to respectfully and freely express their opinions during community forums. When people set aside their disagreements to work together toward a common goal for their community, a turning point is reached.

Through these discussions, they learn to appreciate varying viewpoints, recognizing the value in compromise. They commit to working together, driven by love for their community. The communal spirit evolves, leading to initiatives that promote inclusivity and connection. In this way, love becomes a catalyst for transformation, inspiring people to overcome challenges and find common ground.

As we explore love in these diverse contexts, it is essential to confront the challenges we face in expressing and receiving love. Each setting presents unique obstacles, often rooted in fear, insecurity, or miscommunication. Within families, misunderstandings can erupt into conflicts that threaten relationships. In friendships, unspoken needs and expectations can create distance between people. At work, a lack of empathy or appreciation can make it hard for love and support to grow. In communities, division and prejudice can break connections, hiding the love that should bring everyone together.

Acknowledging these challenges empowers us to confront them directly. Love, at its core, requires vulnerability and strength. In families, open communication can dissolve tensions, replacing hostility with understanding. In friendships, reaching out to those we care about can rekindle bonds that distance has weakened. In workplaces, fostering a culture of respect and support invites collaboration and engagement. In communities, embracing diversity and shared goals can overcome divisions, leading to collective growth.

In the end, love has the power to transform every part of our lives. It helps us build stronger, deeper relationships and connect with others in more meaningful ways. Through shared experiences and emotional investments, we learn that love is not merely a feeling; it is an action. It's about showing up, listening, empathizing, and making a conscious effort to uplift one another.

As we navigate the complexities of love within families, friendships, workplaces, and communities, we may also confront our definitions of love. What does it mean to love unconditionally in these contexts? How can we reflect God's love in our interactions with others? Each of these questions invites deep self-reflection, challenging us to embody love that transcends the expected.

Let us not forget that love is a journey—one that evolves and grows with time. As we face challenges, let us commit to practicing love courageously. When misunderstandings arise in families, may we approach one another with grace. In friendships, when distance threatens to pull us apart, let us reach out. In the workplace, when negativity surfaces, let us choose to encourage one another. In communities, when division arises, let us champion inclusion.

The beauty of love lies in its ability to transform contexts and hearts alike. It teaches us patience, empathy, and the significance of shared experiences. It reminds us that, despite challenges, we can cultivate love in every area of our lives.

As we think about the different ways love shows up in our lives, let's appreciate the stories of connection, growth, and change. Whether it's family moments filled with laughter, friendships that last through the years, teamwork that leads to new ideas at work, or communities coming together for a common purpose, all of these are beautiful examples of love in action.

And as we embrace this transformative journey, may we be empowered to extend love in every context we encounter. Let our love be active, intentional, and reflective of God's unconditional grace, as we become vessels of love in a world that yearns for connection and understanding.

Practical Applications of Love

In our journey to reflect God's love in our lives, it is essential to move beyond mere understanding and into action. The love that God extends to us is meant to flow through us, impacting our relationships with others and transforming our communities. To embody this love, we must recognize the practical applications that can lead us to live out the calling to truly love one another. In this subchapter, we will explore actionable steps that can help us reflect God's love through community service, acts of kindness, and fostering relationships built on love and trust.

To set the stage, let's consider the words of 1 John 3:18: "Dear children, let us not love with words or speech but with actions and in truth." This verse is a poignant reminder that love is not just a sentiment we express; it is a dynamic force that compels us to act. Loving God and loving others are intertwined actions, and the fullness of this love should be evident in our daily lives.

One of the most powerful ways to show God's love is by helping others through community service. There are many ways to serve, and even small acts of kindness can spread and make a big difference in many people's lives. Consider volunteering at a local Red Cross Society or a charity organization. These organizations often rely on the dedication of volunteers to provide essential services to those in need. Engaging in this type of service not only meets the immediate needs of individuals but also sends a powerful message about our shared humanity. When we serve, we proactively choose to embody God's love by feeding the hungry, clothing the naked, and providing support to those who are struggling.

A friend once shared a story about her experience volunteering at a local outreach center. She recalled the first time she walked through the doors, feeling nervous and unsure. But as she started spending time with the people there, her heart began to change. She saw how strong they were, even in tough times. By doing small things, like serving meals and listening to their stories, she began to truly feel God's love in a real and powerful way. This volunteer later reflected that it was not just the service she provided that changed lives, but the love and connection that formed in those moments.

As you consider how to engage in community service, reflect on the following questions:

1. What organizations in your community need support?

2. How can your unique gifts and talents contribute to these services?

3. How might you encourage others to join you in this work?

Acts of kindness are another essential facet of embodying God's love. Kindness is often a small action that can have a significant impact on people's lives. It can be as simple as offering a comforting word to someone who is struggling or surprising a friend with a heartfelt note. Kindness has a way of creating ripples of love, spreading joy and warmth.

We can also seek opportunities to practice kindness in unexpected places. Take a moment to offer genuine compliments to coworkers, help a neighbor with their groceries, or simply smile and greet someone you pass on the street. These small gestures may seem trivial, but they have the potential to brighten a person's day and remind them that they are seen and valued.

A personal story from my past highlights the powerful, unexpected impact of kindness. One day, I randomly decided to pay for the meal of the person behind me at a local snack bar. It was just a simple, kind gesture. As I walked away, I saw their surprised look turn into a warm, thankful smile. A few weeks later, I discovered that this person had been going through a particularly difficult time. They later mentioned that this small act of kindness was a turning point for them, reigniting a sense of hope. The beauty of simple acts is that we may never understand the depth of their significance in someone's life.

Incorporating these acts into your daily routine can create a culture of kindness in your environment. Consider the following reflective questions:

1. What small acts of kindness can you incorporate into your day-to-day life?

2. Are there specific individuals or communities that may need a little extra kindness?

3. How can you challenge yourself to be more aware of moments where you can show love through kindness?

Another essential element in reflecting God's love is fostering relationships built on love and trust. Building strong, meaningful relationships takes time and effort, but the benefits are priceless. In a world that can often feel lonely and disconnected, creating a space filled with trust and love can certainly change lives.

Start by being open and vulnerable with those around you. Trust is built when we allow ourselves to be seen and known. Share your thoughts, dreams, and struggles with those you care about. Create safe spaces for dialogue, where everyone feels heard and valued. This openness fosters deeper relationships and encourages others to reciprocate.

Consider the power of being present in your relationships. Spend quality time with loved ones, free from distractions. Whether it's a weekend gathering or a simple phone call, prioritize moments that foster connection. Listening attentively to someone requires time and effort, but it shows that their thoughts and feelings matter.

An associate Pastor once shared her experiences of creating a close-knit community in her church. She encouraged small groups to meet regularly to share their lives and faith in a deep and meaningful way. These intentional gatherings became a source of strength, allowing individuals to support one another through life's ups and downs. The love present in their interactions became a natural overflow of their commitment to each other and to God.

As you work to build and foster relationships, consider reflecting on these questions:

1. Who in your life could benefit from a deeper relationship with you?

2. How can you create more opportunities for connection and bonding?

3. What barriers exist in your relationships that prevent the growth of love and trust?

In taking these actionable steps, remember that reflecting God's love is not an endpoint but a journey. Each act of service, kindness, and strengthened relationship adds layers to our understanding of love and our capacity to embody it. When we embrace vulnerability and reach toward others with our hearts open, we create a ripple effect that magnifies love in our communities.

It can be tempting to feel overwhelmed by the sheer number of needs and challenges present in our world today. But love doesn't mean we have to do everything or meet every need. It starts with one small act of kindness, one moment of connection, or simply helping someone. These small actions add up, showing the kind of love God has for all people.

As you consider how you can reflect God's love in your own life, it is also valuable to think about creating a personal action plan. This plan can help you stay focused and accountable in your journey. Here are some actionable steps to guide you:

1. Identify Your Gifts: Take time to reflect on your unique talents, passions, and resources. How can you use these gifts to serve others in your community? Write down specific ways you can contribute and the organizations you can collaborate with.

2. Set Achievable Goals: Choose one or two areas where you want to focus your love in practical ways. Set clear, achievable goals for how you will reflect love through community service, acts of kindness, or relationship-building.

3. Schedule Time: Intentional love requires time. Block out specific times in your calendar for service activities, acts of kindness, or quality time with loved ones. Treat these appointments as sacred commitments to yourself and others.

4. Share Your Plan: Let others know your goals. Sharing your intentions creates accountability and allows you to involve friends or family who might want to join you in your efforts to reflect God's love.

5. Reflect and Adjust: Regularly review your action plan. Reflect on what is working and what could use improvement. Be open to adjusting your approach as you grow and learn.

6. By creating a personal action plan, you empower yourself to take tangible steps toward living out your faith. It allows you to move past feelings of inadequacy and into a space of proactive love.

In conclusion, reflecting God's love in our lives is a dynamic calling that invites us to action. The practical applications of community service, acts of kindness, and nurturing relationships strengthen our hearts and communities. Through intentionality and a commitment to love, we pave the way for deeper connections and increased understanding of God's love for us.

May we approach each day with our hearts open to the opportunities presented before us to love actively and meaningfully. It is in these moments of service and kindness, manifested in relationship with one another, that we truly embody the love of God, demonstrating its truth to a world hungry for connection and compassion.

Chapter 6:
The Cost of Love

Understanding Sacrifice

The deepest kind of love is intertwined with sacrifice. It shows itself as a decision to prioritize the needs of another person over our own, which frequently puts us in challenging situations when security and comfort are compromised. The truth that genuine love is more than just a feeling and is an action based on the willingness to give of oneself is revealed to us as we explore the depths of comprehending sacrifice in love, whether it be for God or for others. This is demonstrated by the supreme sacrifice made by Jesus Christ, whose life and death offer a model for how we could live out this difficult yet transforming principle.

From the very beginning of His ministry, Jesus exemplified a life of sacrifice. He lived not for Himself, but for the sake of others. He taught that the greatest commandment is to love God with all one's heart, soul, and mind, but He did not stop there. He added that we must love our neighbors as ourselves (Matthew 22:37-39). This dual command encapsulates the essence of sacrifice. To love God is to align our priorities with His, often at the expense of our own preferences and desires. To love others involves stepping into their shoes, empathizing with their struggles, and sometimes bearing the weight of their burdens alongside them.

In life, we frequently find ourselves at a crossroads where love calls us to make sacrifices. The Seeker, an everyday person dealing with the ups and downs of relationships, often comes across important moments like these. It might be a friend who needs support during an illness, or a family member facing a hardship that calls for the Seeker's time and help. In those moments, the Seeker must confront the uncomfortable question: "What am I willing to give up for the sake of this love?"

This inquiry is not just one of physical resources, though. It often involves mental and emotional sacrifices too. The Seeker recalls the days when he would prioritize his own needs, work deadlines, personal ambitions, and comfort over the needs of those around him. Yet, as he reflects on Jesus' sacrifice, he realizes that love calls him to discomfort. It asks him to set aside his plans and often his comfort zones, embracing the vulnerability that comes with genuinely caring for others.

Throughout scripture, we see countless instances of sacrifice. Abraham was called to leave his homeland, sacrificing the familiarity of his life for the sake of a promise (Genesis 12:1-4). Moses sacrificed his position and privilege in Pharaoh's palace for the sake of his people (Exodus 2:11-15). These acts of forsaking comfort for greater causes show us that sacrifice is a divine attribute.

The ultimate act of sacrifice, however, transcends these historical accounts. John 3:16 reveals that love is not passive or sentimental—it is costly. God's love moved Him to give His Son so humanity could be rescued from perishing and invited into eternal life. If this is the cost God was willing to pay for us, then the question before us is how willing are we to respond to such costly love. Jesus' death on the cross stands as the centerpiece of Christian faith, a profound expression of love that demands our reflection. He bore not just the physical agony of crucifixion but also the weight of humanity's collective failings. In that act of sacrifice, Jesus showed a love so deep that it goes beyond what we can fully understand. It is a love that challenges us to rethink how we relate to God and to one another.

But what does it mean for us, as followers of Christ, to engage in this kind of sacrifice? It requires a willingness to lay down our lives metaphorically, if not literally. To practice sacrificial love, we need to let go of our feelings of entitlement, our desire for ease, and the inclination to guard our time carefully. It compels us to extend grace, to forgive, and to aid others even when it is inconvenient.

Love often requires sacrifice in the form of time. In a world driven by busy schedules and overflowing to-do lists, dedicating time to nurture a relationship can feel burdensome. Yet, this is where true love flourishes. The Seeker understands that time spent with loved ones signifies commitment and care; it becomes a testament to his love. Moments spent listening, laughing, and being present reveal the heartbeat of healthy relationships.

We must face our own hesitation to make sacrifices when dealing with relationships. The Seeker recalls an important time when a close friend was struggling with addiction. The Seeker struggled with whether to devote time and effort to helping this friend, as the journey was stressful with unpredictable ups and downs. It was disconcerting to think of emotional turmoil and possible disappointment. But when the decision was made to remain and provide unwavering love, the Seeker realized that their relationship had become stronger and that they had a deep understanding of sacrificial love.

This story resonates with the broader themes of love expressed in 1 Corinthians 13. Love is patient, love is kind, and it does not insist on its own way (1 Corinthians 13:4-5). Herein lies a blueprint for sacrifice in love, an invitation to prioritize the well-being of others over our momentary feelings of inconvenience or discomfort.

To delve deeper into the concept of sacrifice, we must examine the idea of setting aside our desires for a higher purpose. Sacrificial love is not transactional; it doesn't seek reciprocity. Jesus' sacrifice on the cross was not contingent on humanity's response but was an unconditional offering of love. In relationships, this can translate to loving without keeping score, without insisting that love be returned in the same measure we give it.

The Seeker reflects on moments in his life when he operated from a place of expectation rather than pure love. Each time he anticipated that his kindness would be met with gratitude or that his sacrifice would yield a specific outcome, he limited the possibilities of what love could unfold in those interactions. However, the moments when he acted from a place of unconditional giving, those instances filled with grace and compassion, led to genuine connections and unexpected joys.

Acknowledging that love often demands sacrifice is not meant to instill guilt but to evoke a sense of responsibility. In understanding the cost of love, we are also reminded of the immense benefit it brings, both to ourselves and to those we love. The Seeker finds this truth echoed in the lives of everyday heroes, parents, caregivers, and friends who courageously support those in need. Their sacrifices symbolize a love that is both beautiful and inspiring.

The complexities involved in sacrifice also emerge when we consider the sacrifices we make in the name of God. Following God's calling often means letting go of control and stepping into the unknown. It could involve changing careers, moving to a new place, or serving in a capacity that feels uncomfortable. The Seeker contemplates the divinely inspired callings in scripture, Moses, who reluctantly accepted the mantle of leadership after initially resisting a call to confront Pharaoh, and Jonah, who ran from a mission only to be redirected dramatically. Each story of obedience underscores that God can shape our sacrifices into incredible purposes, turning what feels like loss into immense gain for His kingdom.

It is also crucial to recognize the intrinsic value found in the act of loving sacrificially. While sacrifices will often inconvenience us, they also cultivate spiritual growth. Each time the Seeker pushes past his comfort zones and loves boldly, he finds himself becoming more like Christ, embodying the character of the One who loved him first. This process unfolds in moments of vulnerability, where the truth of God's love penetrates the depths of his heart, igniting a passion to share that same love with others. Yet the struggle to sacrifice is still there. The Seeker wrestles with moments of hesitation and doubt, when sacrifice feels heavy and the fear of being unappreciated grows strong. In these moments, he is reminded of the words of Paul: "For I consider that the sufferings of this present time are not worth comparing with the glory that is to be revealed to us" (Romans 8:18). There is solace in understanding that the challenges faced in making sacrifices for love are not in vain; they are seeds planted within the soil of God's greater plan.

The beauty of sacrificial love is that it often leads to immense joy and fulfillment to both the giver and the recipient. The Seeker discovers the powerful truth that love creates more love, setting off a ripple effect that encourages more kindness and compassion. He realizes that when he steps out to meet someone else's needs, he doesn't lose anything himself; instead, he gains a deeper understanding of both love and community. The journey of loving sacrificially transforms him, expanding his capacity to love and teaching him to embrace the mutual dependence in relationships.

As we consider the broader implications of love in sacrifice, we should also reflect on how to cultivate an environment that fosters sacrificial love.

It begins with community, the willingness of those within our circles to encourage and spur one another on in their journeys. As the Seeker navigates his relationships, he seeks accountability and encouragement among friends who share a commitment to love sacrificially. This communal approach underscores the essence of the body of Christ, where each member plays a part in uplifting one another, supporting sacrifices made out of love.

The Seeker discovers tangible ways to implement sacrificial love within his community: volunteering time at local community centers, organizing events that promote togetherness, and reaching out to those who feel isolated or alone. These actions draw him closer to both God and others, revealing the power of love that transcends individual desire.

As we draw this exploration of sacrifice to a conclusion, it becomes increasingly clear that understanding sacrifice is foundational to our journey in love. Love requires us to examine our own motivations, surrender our desires, and embrace discomfort for the sake of connection. Each act of sacrifice, no matter how small, contributes to the richness of our relationships, painting a broader picture of what it means to embody Christ's love.

The invitation for all of us is to step courageously into this journey of sacrificial love, knowing that even when it costs us something, the rewards can be eternal. As we remember the ultimate sacrifice made for us, we too are called to offer ourselves, for love, for God, and for each other. The Seeker's story is a reminder of the transformative power that unfolds when we choose to love freely, unreservedly embracing the cost of love in our lives.

Examples of Sacrificial Love

In a world that often prioritizes personal gain and individualism, the stories of sacrificial love stand as powerful reminders of the profound impact that selflessness can have on individuals and communities alike. Sacrificial love, by its very nature, demands a cost, whether it be time, resources, or personal comfort. By examining biblical narratives and real-life examples of this love, we can gain not only an understanding of what it means to truly love, but also how to apply these lessons in our own lives.

The parable of the Good Samaritan is one of the most renowned examples of sacrificial love found in Scripture. In the Gospel of Luke, Jesus uses this story to challenge societal norms and illustrate the true essence of love. Robbers brutally attack a man traveling from Jerusalem to Jericho, left to suffer on the side of the road. First, a priest and then a Levite, walked past the wounded man, choosing not to stop and help. Their actions showed a decision to prioritize their own comfort and status instead of caring for someone in need.

It is not until a Samaritan approaches that we see the embodiment of sacrificial love. The Samaritans, historically regarded with contempt by the Jews, defy expectations. Moved by compassion, the Samaritan tends to the wounded man's injuries, using his own resources to care for him. He takes him to an inn, pays for his care, and promises to return to cover any additional expenses. This story exemplifies several forms of sacrificial love: physical care, financial support, emotional investment, and the willingness to challenge societal norms for the sake of another.

Considering how the Samaritan's actions disrupted his routine, he could have easily justified walking past the injured man, citing his own needs or potential social stigmas. Yet, he chose to elevate the needs of the suffering over his own comfort. This bears a striking resemblance to the modern-day examples of sacrificial love that continue to emerge across various contexts.

Mother Teresa provides another compelling illustration of sacrificial love in action. Known for her unwavering commitment to the poorest of the poor in Calcutta, India, she dedicated her life to serving those who were marginalized, sick, and dying. With little regard for her own safety or comfort, she lived among those whom society had cast aside, embodying the love of Christ in her relentless service.

Mother Teresa once stated, "Not all of us can do great things. But we can do small things with great love." Her words resonate deeply, underscoring that sacrificial love does not always manifest in grand gestures. Rather, it can be found in seemingly small acts of kindness—a loving smile, a gentle touch, or a listening ear, to someone in desperate need. Through her Sisters of Charity, she established hospices and homes for the dying, providing a place for individuals to experience love and dignity in their final days.

The depth of her sacrificial love is evident in the time she spent with those in despair. She did not simply provide material support; she offered companionship, compassion, and a sense of belonging. Her life reminds us that selflessness and humanity meet in sacrificial love. It challenges us to consider our own lives: Are we willing to share our time, resources, and hearts with those in need, just as the Good Samaritan and Mother Teresa did?

As we explore modern examples, we can look to everyday heroes, people within our communities who embody sacrificial love through acts of kindness and service. Consider a local firefighter who goes above and beyond, risking his life to save another during a treacherous blaze. Or a teacher who devotes countless hours to ensuring that her students, many of whom come from challenging backgrounds, receive not only an education but also the encouragement and warmth they need to thrive. In both instances, these individuals choose to put the needs of others before their own comfort.

Volunteers who commit their time to mentoring at-risk youths or serving food to the less fortunate are also examples of such acts of kindness. They understand that even the smallest of their contributions can have a profound impact on others, changing lives in their wake. Sacrificial love is evident in each of these situations, serving as a reminder that love has a price. It necessitates giving up one's own time, resources, and, occasionally, even safety, in order to prioritize the welfare of others.

To further the understanding of sacrificial love, we can draw insight from the parable of the Sheep and the Goats found in Matthew 25:31-46. In this passage, Jesus vividly illustrates the importance of serving others, declaring that whatever is done for the "least of these" is done for Him. This teaching underscores the practical nature of love; it's not merely a feeling but a call to action. When we choose to care for the hungry, the thirsty, the stranger, the naked, the sick, and the imprisoned, we are engaging in acts of sacrificial love that reverberate throughout the Kingdom of God.

Each of us has the capacity to practice sacrificial love in our daily lives. It requires intentionality and a willingness to step outside our comfort zones. Reflect for a moment on your own community: Are there individuals or groups you might overlook? Perhaps seniors who might need companionship, struggling families who could benefit from a meal, or children in need of mentorship? The need for sacrificial love is pervasive, and there's no shortage of opportunities to practice it.

By embracing a mindset of sacrificial love, we can become catalysts for change within our communities. This does not mean that every act of love must come with a monumentally high cost, but rather that we recognize the value in every gesture, whether big or small. Whether it's offering your time to listen, your resources to assist, or your hands to serve, we exemplify God's love through our actions.

In a letter to the Corinthians, the Apostle Paul emphasizes the importance of love, stating, "And now these three remain: faith, hope, and love. But the greatest of these is love" (1 Corinthians 13:13). Love governs our actions and defines our responses to the world around us. It transcends personal sacrifice, offering a pathway to healing and connection.

As we reflect on our own journeys, we might look to those who have influenced us through their acts of sacrificial love. These individuals might not have worn capes or held famous titles, but their influence has been vast. It could have been a grandparent who cared for you during tough times or a friend who sat with you quietly during your lowest moments. Acts of love, especially during hardship, offer comfort and exemplify the arms of God wrapping around us.

The call to sacrificial love is not limited to individual actions; it extends into community initiatives and collective endeavors. For instance, consider the powerful movement of communities coming together for a common cause, such as disaster relief efforts during natural disasters. These initiatives exemplify the power of sacrificial love when individuals pool their resources, time, and energy to support those affected.

Furthermore, we see sacrificial love manifested when local congregations respond to the needs of their neighborhoods, providing food pantries, tutoring programs, or outreach ministries that seek to uplift others. Within these communal efforts, the cost of love may involve financial contributions or personal sacrifices of time, but the collective impact is significant. Each participant embodies Christ's love, showcasing the transformative power of coming together to serve.

As we engage with the narrative of sacrificial love, let us not become passive observers. Instead, we are tasked with the challenge of actively seeking opportunities to embody this love. Reflect on your values and beliefs. How do they influence your understanding of what it means to love sacrificially? Reflect on the ways you live out your faith and consider how you might bring more intentionality to your actions.

It is through small, consistent acts that the foundation of sacrificial love is laid. These moments may go unnoticed or might seem insignificant, yet they contribute to a culture of love that promotes healing and restoration. Perhaps it is as simple as checking in with a neighbor, volunteering time at a local charity, or making a donation to support those in need. Each act, no matter how small, breeds hope and lights the way for others.

Finally, as we continue to reflect on our own capacity for sacrificial love, let us remember the ultimate example set before us by Jesus Christ. Jesus' life was a perfect example of selfless love, as He gave His life for humanity, a powerful sacrifice that continues to impact us today. He didn't just talk about love; He lived it, giving us the greatest gift of all.

In light of Christ's example, we are called to act as conduits of His love, extending that love to others through our own sacrifices. Each instance of sacrificial love we enact not only reflects God's heart but also brings us closer to understanding the depth of His love for us.

Take a moment to reflect on your life. Notice where you may be hesitant to act and invite God into those spaces. Allow Him to lead you in making paths of sacrificial love that echo His own. Love indeed costs something, but the return on that investment transcends all comprehensible value; it births hope, inspires others, and brings glory to the One who first loved us.

When we choose sacrificial love, we step into a journey of growth, healing, and building stronger communities. As we move forward, let the stories of the Good Samaritan, Mother Teresa, and contemporary heroes inspire us to keep going, committing ourselves to love that touches lives, strengthens communities, and reflects the very heart of God.

The Joy in Sacrifice

Love often shines brightest in moments of sacrifice. Sacrifice isn't easy; it costs us something personal, and it can feel heavy to carry. Yet, it's in those very moments that we uncover the truest meaning of love: a joy that comes from connection, purpose, and giving of ourselves. When we choose to let go of a little for the sake of others, we not only help transform their lives but also discover a transformation within our own.

As the Mentor sat with the Seeker, a gentle breeze whispered through the open windows of the café where they often convened. They were surrounded by the hum of conversations, laughter, and the comforting aroma of freshly brewed coffee. The Seeker had been contemplating sacrifice, feeling the weight of the world upon his shoulders. It was in his discontent that he found curiosity; if sacrifice is heavy, then what joy could possibly exist on the other side?

"Sacrifice can often feel like a burden," the Mentor began, placing a warm, comforting hand over the Seeker's. "But it is essential to understand that within each act of sacrificial love lies the potential for tremendous joy and fulfillment. Have you ever experienced a moment where giving something away, the last piece of your cake, a part of your time, or your heart, brought you joy?"

The Seeker pondered, recollecting instances of generosity that left him feeling both contented and exhilarated. "I remember volunteering at a local outreach event last year," he replied. "I brought food and spent time with the people there. It felt good to help, yet I often felt exhausted by the end of the day."

The Mentor nodded knowingly. "That exhaustion is part of the cost, yes. Sacrifice ties into the very core of love, where our comfort can sometimes take a backseat. But the joy, oh, the joy that comes from knowing you've touched someone else's life! It's a glimpse of how God loves us, don't you think?"

"Maybe," the Seeker replied hesitantly, still grappling with the concept. "But how do we reconcile the heaviness of sacrifice with the joy you're speaking of?"

"Let's reflect on some stories," the Mentor proposed, leaning forward. "These are not just tales; they are testimonies of individuals who have discovered joy in the act of giving. They reveal how the simplest sacrifices can lead to the most profound connections..."

There was a woman named Karen, who dedicated her weekends to visiting the elderly in nursing homes. Initially, she went mostly out of duty, joining a church outreach program she felt obligated to be part of. She would show up, engage in small talk, and listen politely to the stories of those who had lived long lives. At first, she regarded her participation as a sacrifice of her personal free time, especially since her weekends were precious. But as time passed, she began to notice a change within herself.

During one visit, Karen met Mrs. Thompson, who spoke of her youth, her dreams, and her regrets. It was a heart-wrenching but beautiful glimpse into a life saturated with both pain and joy. As she listened, Karen felt an overwhelming connection, an invisible thread of love weaving between them. Somewhere in the midst of listening, she realized she was not merely giving her time; she was allowing her heart to break open, to be enriched by another's experiences.

It was as if Mrs. Thompson's stories filled a reservoir of joy within Karen, a joy born from connection, empathy, and understanding. She began to look forward to her visits, not out of obligation, but out of genuine love for the people she met there. Each sacrifice of her time became an offering that filled her spirit, driving her to serve even more.

"In giving, Karen found her purpose," the Mentor remarked. "She discovered that through her willingness to step out from her comfort zone and invest in others, she became part of something larger than herself. That's the joy that arises from sacrificial love."

The Seeker nodded thoughtfully, allowing Karen's story to sink in. "It's almost as if the giving allows for a deeper connection. It's no longer just about doing something; it's about belonging."

"Precisely!" the Mentor exclaimed, excitedly leaning forward. "When we love sacrificially, we step into a realm of communion with others and with God. We reflect the very essence of love that God has for us, a love that does not shy away from sacrifice."

Consider the example of a father named David, who worked long hours to provide for his family. He often missed playing catch with his son or attending his daughter's dance recitals. The emotional toll weighed heavy on him, and his heart ached for the moments he had sacrificed for the sake of their future.

One day, after much contemplation, he realized that he could still create moments despite the busyness of life. He decided to rearrange his priorities, making a conscious effort to show up for his children. With each occasion he chose to forego a business meeting or work overtime, he was met with laughter and light in their eyes.

In those moments, as David sacrificed his pride and work demands, he discovered a deeper fulfillment—the joy of connection with his children. The smiles and laughter replaced his exhaustion with a renewed sense of purpose. He felt a fire reignite within him as he recognized that the happiness in their faces was worth more than any award he could achieve in his professional life.

"David's joy came from the intimacy he built with his children," the Mentor explained. "It exemplifies how sacrificial love fosters relationships that transcend mere duty. Each moment spent together no longer felt like a sacrifice, but a gift yielding abundance."

The Seeker couldn't help but connect the dots. "It seems that the joy of sacrifice is not solely about what we give up, but about what we gain: connection, love, and community."

"Beautifully said," the Mentor responded. "When we embrace the cost of love, we open ourselves up to experiences that are rich and transformative, not just for others, but for ourselves. Can you recall a time when you felt joy from making a sacrifice for someone else?"

The Seeker leaned back, allowing memories to replay like a film in his mind. "I remember a season when my friend was going through a difficult time. I took time off work to help her pack her things and move. It was exhausting, but somehow… I felt like I was exactly where I needed to be. Supporting her, cheering her on, it felt rewarding."

A smile spread across the Mentor's face. "That's sacrificial love! You surrendered your time and energy to lift someone else up, which ultimately deepened your bond with her. This is what creates belonging, a sense that you are part of something larger and that your sacrifices matter."

Reflecting on that sentiment, the Seeker felt a warmth spread through him. "It's exhilarating to think that in our willingness to share our burdens and engage with others, we discover our own joy. But sacrifice can still feel daunting at times."

The Mentor's eyes sparkled knowingly. "Indeed, it can. The path of sacrificial love is not without its challenges. Yet, it's essential to recognize that the initial discomfort often gives way to a joy that reinforces our purpose. It's in the midst of our struggles where we often experience God's love blossoming through us.

Consider the story of Alyssa, who experienced loss during a challenging season of her life. After her sister's passing, she sank into an abyss of sorrow, overwhelmed by grief. In her pain, she felt disconnected from everyone, questioning how to move forward.

One day, she decided to volunteer at a grief support group. At first, it was difficult for her to step into a place where she would witness others grappling with pain similar to her own. Yet, as Alyssa listened to the stories of others sharing their struggles, she felt a profound sense of belonging.

By sacrificing her evenings to support others in their grieving process, she found solace and joy amidst her sorrow. It was within those shared experiences of pain and healing that she connected deeply not only with those she served but also with herself. As she offered understanding, she discovered her own wounds began to heal. Her sacrifices, once painful reminders of what she had lost, transformed into a testament of resilience and love.

"Alyssa's story illustrates that sacrificial love has the power to heal not only ourselves but also those around us," the Mentor said softly, echoing the sentiment of interconnection. "In lifting one another, we find that our burdens are lighter and our joys are more abundant."

The Seeker contemplated Alyssa's journey, feeling his heart swell at the thought. "So, in our sacrifices, we create a new narrative, a story of healing and empowerment. That's incredibly powerful."

"Yes, and it's imperative to recognize that our journey toward joy through sacrifice is continual," the Mentor said, encouraging the Seeker to reflect further. "To navigate this path, we must be willing to embrace discomfort, uncertainty, and vulnerability. These are the very textures of sacrificial love that lead us to profound transformation."

As you embark on loving sacrificially, I encourage you to ask yourself: What joy might arise from stepping outside your comfort zone? Are there relationships in your life where love could be deepened through your willingness to sacrifice?"

The Seeker smiled, feeling an invitation to reflect. "I suppose I can think about small things I can do for my family and friends, maybe taking the time to really listen, or help with little tasks that can lighten their load."

"Perfect!" the Mentor said enthusiastically. "Joy often bursts forth from the tiniest acts of love. Each moment you choose to serve another, you embody the heart of God, who is ever-present in our love for one another. Remember, sacrifice doesn't have to be grand; it can be simple gestures that make the world a little brighter for someone else."

After an hour of heartfelt reflection on shared experiences, they rose to leave. The Seeker felt a sense of reassurance and purpose, as if the weight of his sorrow had been lifted. He walked away with a new understanding of love, that the joy found in sacrificial love spreads outward, touching many lives and, in the end, guiding us all home.

As the Mentor and Seeker stood up to depart, the conversation gently shifted toward the idea of how they could intentionally create opportunities for love and connection in their daily lives. "This week, challenge yourself to make a small sacrifice, perhaps give time to a neighbor, lend a listening ear to a friend, or support a cause you are passionate about. Document how it feels and the joys you experience as you engage in these acts of love."

The Seeker's eyes sparkled with anticipation. "I'll do it! I can't wait to see what unfolds. The idea of planting seeds of love through sacrifice feels inspiring. Thank you for guiding me."

The Mentor smiled, filled with hope for the journey ahead, knowing that the joy of sacrificial love awaited the Seeker just beyond their next steps.

As they walked out into the world bathed in warm sunlight, each felt their hearts widen with gratitude. Sacrifice is not simply about what we give; it's about what we gain, fulfillment, belonging, and above all, joy rooted in love. For every act, no matter how small, is a testament to the sacred connection we share, reflecting the boundless love of God that calls us to each other.

As you, dear reader, reflect on your own life and the sacrifices you are called to make, may you embrace this journey with open arms, knowing that with each act of love, you too can discover the joy that comes from giving yourself away.

Chapter 7:
Love In Action

Manifesting Love in Daily Life

As the sun peeked through the curtain, casting golden rays across a room that held both promise and chaos, the Seeker sat on the edge of the bed, contemplating the day ahead. Love was indeed the main theme of his life's journey, and as the weight of the world pressed down, a question quietly surfaced in his mind: How can I manifest love in my daily life?

The journey really starts in the little moments of our lives that call us to embody love in its many forms. Love is like a thread that connects us all, woven through everything we share with one another. But the real challenge is figuring out how to turn this deep feeling into real actions, things that make life better for the people around us.

At home, love can be reflected in the mundane tasks that sometimes seem burdensome. The Seeker recalled times when his wife had returned home exhausted from work. Instead of just going through the usual motions, where busy schedules get in the way of connecting, he decided to take a different approach. A simple meal, prepared without any fuss, but with intent, transformed the atmosphere. The Seeker chopped vegetables for a vibrant stir-fry, allowing the aroma to fill the kitchen, a sensory invitation to sit, talk, and connect. As his wife walked through the door, the warmth of the meal and the inviting setting spoke volumes. The act of cooking became not merely a chore but a love letter written in garlic and ginger, a gesture of care and acknowledgment.

It is often in these seemingly small actions that love manifests profoundly. Even small gestures, like making the bed, can show love. When we smooth the sheets or fluff a pillow, we're really caring for the people we love. These little tasks are ways to say "I love you" without using words. When love is infused into our everyday routine, it transforms the ordinary into the extraordinary. The Seeker, with each passing day, became more aware of these moments of possibility.

In the workplace, love may sometimes feel like a scarce resource, overshadowed by deadlines and projects that demand our undivided attention. Yet, it is precisely within this context that love has the power to foster a more cohesive and compassionate environment. The Seeker noticed a colleague struggling with a heavy workload. Instead of focusing solely on his own tasks, he took a moment to pause and reflect on how he could inject kindness into the day. He approached the colleague, offering assistance with a specific task that could lighten the load. This small act not only brought relief to the overburdened coworker but also fostered a sense of camaraderie between them.

As the Seeker went through his workday, he realized that being present for others was an inspiring act of love. A listening ear granted to a coworker who needed to vent, or a simple note of appreciation for someone's effort, can create ripples of positivity that transcend the corporate walls. Love in the workplace cultivates an atmosphere of trust and collaboration, allowing creativity and productivity to flourish. Through these gestures, the Seeker learned that love in action isn't just grand proclamations; it thrives in the everyday encounters that make up the nine-to-five grind.

Communities provide us with another place where love can grow. The Seeker began to notice the people around him: families, elderly neighbors, children playing in the yard, and newcomers trying to find their place. Thinking about being part of this community lit a spark in him, making him want to build real connections.

One bright Saturday morning, the Seeker decided to organize a casual potluck in the local park. He reached out to neighbors, inviting them to come together to share food and stories. The potluck became an emblem of community love, where dishes shared served as a testament to the cultural diversity that enriched their neighborhood. Under the cool shade of the flamboyant tree's branches, laughter mingled with the scents of grilled chicken, vegetables, and baked goods, as an organic interaction progressed through food, friendship, and a shared sense of belonging.

During this gathering, the Seeker took the opportunity to connect deeply with the neighbors. He heard stories of sacrifice, resilience, and joy experienced in the richness of shared humanity. The act of creating such a space fostered a sense of unity and love, transforming mere acquaintances into friends and support systems that would echo the very fabric of their community life.

However, love is not always seamless. The Seeker found hurdles in his pursuit of love in daily life. It was easy to get caught up in the busyness of schedules and forget to call a friend or check on a neighbor in need. Sometimes he struggled inside, and reaching out felt hard. He worried about being rejected, about showing weakness, or was simply held back by fear. But each small step he took with purpose taught him that love often requires us to confront our insecurities, doubts, and fears.

There were days when the Seeker's heart sank as he scanned a list of things to do and realized how easy it was to let love become an afterthought. On one occasion, a series of missed connections weighed heavily on him. He promised to check in on an old friend, but days turned into weeks. That night, self-reflection prompted the need for change. The Seeker sat down with his daily planner and began drafting regular reminders for outreach: a text, a phone call, or a handwritten note.

Embracing love as a daily practice involves intention, self-forgiveness, and accountability. Understanding that love may often come with setbacks allows for a more forgiving relationship with oneself. Learning to navigate these ups and downs instilled resilience and encouraged the Seeker to keep the heart open, regardless of the previous missteps.

Incorporating acts of love into one's routine also necessitates creativity and mindfulness. The Seeker began experimenting with various ways to express love through spontaneous acts, such as leaving little notes in unexpected places, anonymously leaving small gifts on doorsteps, or engaging in random acts of kindness, like paying the tab for someone in a café. Each act cultivated a connection to both the giver and the receiver, illustrating how love comes alive with action.

One particularly meaningful instance occurred when the Seeker decided to leave flowers on the doorstep of a neighbor going through a tough time. With each bloom arranged in a small bouquet, a loving outreach was accompanied by a note that read, "Thinking of you today." The response he received was unbelievable tears of gratitude, heartfelt appreciation, and an invitation to discuss what was weighing heavily on their hearts. Love, in that moment, took root in vulnerability and openness.

Fostering a continuous practice of kindness also calls for moments of reflection to pause and understand the impact love has had in one's life. The Seeker dedicated time each week to journaling his experiences, creating a narrative marked by acts of love, recognizing how each encounter radiated warmth and connection. He also reflected on moments he wished he had acted differently, choosing not to dwell on missed opportunities but focusing on the lessons learned.

As the Seeker wrote in his journal, his view of love began to change. He saw that love was more than just a feeling; it was a call to action. Each page reflected how life could be transformed by love: by being present, showing care, and choosing compassion for both oneself and others.

The Seeker broadened his view to recognize love beyond interpersonal relationships. He noticed how small decisions, such as selecting products that promote sustainability or supporting local businesses, can also be acts of love directed towards the community and the Earth. Each thoughtful choice echoed back the ideals of care and compassion, reflecting a broader love that encompasses all beings.

Living with love each day means balancing what we plan with what comes naturally. It is rooted in making conscious choices that amplify connection while also being open to the unexpected moments where love can emerge organically. Love is undoubtedly a continuous practice, one that invites both joy and challenge. The Seeker embraced the notion that these efforts need not be perfect to be valued. Each step forward crystallized the understanding that every effort made in love reflects the heart of God, inspiring others to do the same.

In the heart of daily existence lies a profound truth: love is not merely a passive concept, but an active force that can drive positivity, healing, and connection. By consciously choosing to embody love in our daily routines, whether at home, in the workplace, or within the confines of our communities, we lay the foundation for transforming both ourselves and those around us.

At the end of the day, as the Seeker lay in bed, he thought about the small victories, the simple moments when love had shown itself in ways that truly mattered. It became clear that the heart of love extends infinitely beyond personal connections; it beckons us to express kindness and compassion towards all, creating a world where love is not just a sentiment but an enduring action, a legacy we pass on.

With the intention of nurturing this practice of love firmly rooted within, the Seeker resolved to continue striving, forgiving his setbacks along the way. He realized that love is dynamic, always changing, and more like a journey than a fixed thing. Each day gives a new chance to show love, and when we do, it spreads outward, touching people's lives and even whole communities. Through intentional acts and reflective practices, the Seeker found himself on a lifelong path, where love knew no bounds, continuously revealing itself in the intricate dance of daily life.

Creating Love-Filled Spaces

Creating love-filled spaces starts with understanding that our environment greatly influences our thoughts, emotions, and interactions. Whether it's a cozy corner in our homes, an office bustling with colleagues, or a community gathering place, each space has the potential to resonate with the love of God. When we cultivate environments that reflect His love, we create havens where hearts can flourish, conversations can deepen, and connections can thrive.

To create a love-filled space, one must start by examining the physical environment. The place we inhabit plays a crucial role in how we feel and how we interact with others. A cluttered and disorganized space can lead to stress and distraction, while an orderly and inviting area can foster peace and harmony. The Mentor, a wise figure who has navigated the ups and downs of building love-filled spaces, often emphasizes the importance of intentionality in arranging our surroundings.

Consider your home. Is it a sanctuary that welcomes families and friends with open arms? The Mentor encourages readers to reflect on their living spaces, with a focus on creating areas that inspire love and connection. This might mean dedicating a room or corner to foster togetherness, filled with comfortable seating, warm lighting, and inviting decorations. Such choices send a welcoming message that says, "This is a place of acceptance and love."

As the Mentor recalls her journey, she shares insights on how small changes can lead to significant impact. She recommends incorporating meaningful symbols of love, such as pictures of family, inspirational quotes, or artwork that evokes positivity and peace. These elements serve as constant reminders of what love looks like, making it easier for those who enter the space to engage with one another and feel at home.

Beyond the physical, emotional spaces are just as vital to nurturing love. These spaces thrive on open communication and support, requiring intentional coordination. The Mentor emphasizes that love flourishes when individuals feel safe sharing their thoughts and feelings without fear of judgment. To foster this kind of atmosphere, it is essential to establish ground rules that encourage honesty, active listening, and respect among all participants in conversations.

Consider a family dinner or a small gathering with friends. How often do we rush through such moments, distracted by our phones or preoccupied with unrelated thoughts? The Mentor encourages setting aside such distractions, implementing "no phone zones" or designated times for unplugging. Being fully present allows for connection and deep relationship-building, qualities that reflect God's love.

Creating emotional spaces involves not only the environment but also the attitudes we adopt towards one another. The Mentor shares a powerful practice: setting intentions before gatherings. This might be a short prayer or a quiet moment to reflect, helping everyone focus on love and kindness during their time together. These simple practices welcome God into the moment and create space for love to grow.

The workplaces also deserve special attention in our quest for love-filled environments. As the Mentor wisely points out, work can often become a place of stress and competition, overshadowing the potential for camaraderie and support. To counteract this, the Mentor suggests fostering a culture of gratitude and recognition within teams. Encouraging colleagues to acknowledge one another's contributions fosters an environment in which everyone feels valued and appreciated.

Implementing team-building activities or moments of shared reflection can serve as powerful reminders of the importance of love in the workplace. The Mentor explains how simple acts—such as celebrating milestones, offering support during challenging times, or just sharing a meal together—can transform work relationships from transactional to relational, mirroring the love God extends to each of us.

In addition to workplaces and homes, community spaces are essential for nurturing love. The Mentor reflects on her experiences with local organizations and ministries, explaining how these environments can become powerful catalysts for change when filled with love. Hosting events, workshops, or gatherings that prioritize love, inclusivity, and support can transform ordinary spaces into transformative hubs where connections flourish.

Think about your local church, a community center, or a park where neighbors gather. Are these places thriving with love, or have they become mere transactional spaces? The Mentor encourages readers to engage with these environments actively. Volunteer to organize events that demonstrate the love of God, such as outreach projects, charity drives, or communal meals. These initiatives invite others to experience love in action while simultaneously building deep bonds within the community.

As you reflect on your own spaces, both physical and emotional, consider the people who enter them. Each individual brings their unique story, experiences, and energy. The Mentor highlights the importance of viewing these encounters as divinely orchestrated opportunities for love. This mindset can shape the way we interact with others, prompting us to extend hospitality to strangers, invite in those who differ from us, and create relationships that transcend boundaries.

Creating and nurturing love-filled spaces require vulnerability and intentionality. The Mentor shares her own struggles in this process, acknowledging that building environments of love isn't always easy. There are times when misunderstandings, miscommunications, or conflicts can arise, threatening to undermine the intended atmosphere. In those moments, the Mentor emphasizes the importance of patience, grace, and forgiveness.

When conflicts arise, it is crucial to address them directly yet compassionately. Understanding that disagreements are a natural part of any relationship allows individuals to navigate them with a mindset rooted in love. Using techniques learned from the Mentor, readers can approach difficult conversations with empathy, listening closely to one another, and seeking common ground.

Equally important is the practice of gratitude in maintaining love-filled spaces. The Mentor encourages a culture of appreciation, sharing how expressing gratitude can magnify the love we cultivate. Simple expressions of thanks or recognition go a long way in reinforcing a sense of belonging and importance. Just as God pours His love into our lives, we should reflect that love by honoring those who walk alongside us on our journey.

To nurture gratitude together, consider organizing ceremonies or family traditions that honor the contributions of each member. The Mentor shares the story of a family that hosts an annual "gratitude night," where each person takes turns sharing something they love about others in their family. This practice not only strengthens connections but also creates an environment drenched in appreciation and warmth.

As we work to create spaces filled with love, we must not overlook the importance of ongoing reflection and adjustment. It is essential to regularly assess the environment we create and be open to making necessary changes. The Mentor encourages us to set aside dedicated time to look at our spaces with care. This could be through journaling, prayer, or talking with loved ones. By noticing where more love can grow, we strengthen our relationships and stay attentive to the needs of everyone who shares the space.

In this process of evaluating and shaping our love-filled spaces, we invite the Holy Spirit into our journey, seeking His guidance in creating the environments that truly reflect God's love. The Mentor reminds us that prayer plays a crucial role in this endeavor. By asking God to help us build and maintain these spaces, we open ourselves to divine wisdom and insight that enrich our interactions and foster greater love among all.

As you think about your role in creating love-filled spaces, it's important to recognize that you might not be able to change the entire environment overnight. Instead, focus on small adjustments that match your vision of love. This gradual approach can lead to meaningful changes over time, as God works through these efforts to touch lives and build relationships.

Finally, remember that the journey to creating love-filled spaces is ongoing. It's a dynamic process requiring commitment, dedication, and a willingness to learn and grow. The Mentor's journey illustrates that while it may not always be easy, the rewards of fostering environments brimming with love are immeasurable, both for ourselves and for those who enter our spaces.

Take a moment now to reflect on your spaces. What is one change you can make today to invite love more profoundly into your life and the lives of others? Whether it is rearranging a room, opening your home for connection, or implementing practices in your workplace that emphasize gratitude and support, remember that each step forward invites the overwhelming, never-ending love of God into the foundation of our lives. By doing so, we enable ourselves and others to experience the transformative power of love in action.

Community Engagement and Service

Service is often described as the heart of love in action, a tangible expression of the unconditional, overwhelming love that God offers us. In a world where individualism often reigns supreme, engaging with our communities through service invites us to step outside ourselves and embrace the collective human experience. It creates opportunities for connection, nurture, and understanding, elements that are crucial not only for personal growth but for the flourishing of society as a whole.

As we explore the many ways we can engage in community service, let us first remember the core principle that unites this act: love. The purpose of love isn't just to meet others' needs; it is to build relationships that foster hope, joy, and connection. Love expressed through community service reminds us that no one should be left behind, that everyone deserves dignity, and that our shared humanity calls us to action.

The Seeker, in his journey, has witnessed the transformative power of love that is fostered through shared experiences of service. He began as a mere participant, motivated by obligation rather than a deeper sense of purpose. However, as he engaged more deeply with his community, he discovered that giving back was much more than about helping those in need; it became a source of fulfillment, connection, and growth.

In this narrative, the Seeker volunteered with a local food charity. Initially, he approached the experience with a simple mindset: "I have to do this because it's the right thing to do." Yet, something shifted as he entered the bustling warehouse. Amid the chatter of volunteers sorting through boxes of food, a palpable spirit of camaraderie emerged. Each person was not merely a name on a roster; they were souls united by a heartfelt motivation to serve their neighbors and share love through the act of providing nourishment.

Over the weeks, the Seeker found himself not only distributing food but also sharing stories, laughter, and moments of vulnerability with fellow volunteers. He realized that in every interaction, he was reinforcing the bonds of love between neighbors, between strangers, and within himself. Witnessing the joy on the faces of those receiving assistance illuminated the impact of their collective efforts, and a sense of purpose began to flourish in his heart.

Community service, as showcased through the Seeker's journey, fosters deeper connections. It transcends mere obligation or duty; it evolves into a sacred act of presence, compassion, and empathy. When we engage in our communities, we participate in a shared narrative that uplifts not only those we serve but also ourselves. Each act of kindness creates ripples that reach into lives far beyond our initial intention. In giving, we receive; in serving, we grow.

To immerse ourselves in the spirit of service, we must consider the many avenues available for community engagement. There are infinite possibilities, each tailored to unique abilities, interests, and circumstances. By participating, we can explore various facets of love in action.

One powerful way to engage is through mentorship programs, which can have a lasting impact on individuals, especially the youth. Imagine sharing your skills, knowledge, and experiences with someone eager to learn. You create a relationship that helps both of you to grow. Mentorship becomes a two-way exchange, where guidance inspires potential and encourages dreams.

Consider a local school that seeks volunteers to assist students struggling in math or reading. As a mentor, you would not only help improve their academic performance but also inspire confidence and ambition in them. The Seeker reflects on his time spent volunteering at the school and remembers how completely transformed both his life and the lives of those he mentored became because of mutual effort and commitment. He remembers the sparkle in a young student's eye when he solved a math problem correctly for the first time. In that moment, success wasn't just numerical; it was a blossoming identity birthed from love and support.

Another dimension of community service lies in engaging with the arts. Serving at or supporting local art organizations elevates the value of creativity and expression in our neighborhoods. Art is extremely powerful, it has the ability to provoke thought, spark dialogue, and create deeper understandings of one another. The Seeker recalls his time volunteering at an after-school arts program, where kids came alive with creativity. As they collaborated to create stunning paintings together, the young artists learned more than just techniques; they also learned to trust openly, express vulnerability, and embrace their uniqueness within a diverse community.

Connecting with those who are differently abled is yet another avenue of love in action. The Seeker discovered a local organization fostering inclusion and support for individuals with disabilities. Engaging with this community instilled a deeper understanding of resilience in the Seeker. He learned that love and companionship are not defined by physical ability but by empathy, patience, and kindness. Each moment spent together highlighted the beauty of human connections formed through shared smiles, laughter, and support.

Environmental stewardship is also a critical aspect of community service. The Seeker learned that an integral part of loving others is loving our planet. Participating in local clean-up initiatives not only preserves the beauty of God's creation but also fosters teamwork and community pride. He recalls an experience where a group of volunteers gathered for a park restoration project. Together, they cleaned up litter, planted trees, and laughed heartily as they worked side by side. These seemingly small acts merged into a grand act of stewardship that contributed significantly to the lives of both people and the environment, reminding everyone that love for our planet has a cascading effect on our communities.

As he navigated through various service opportunities, the Seeker began to reflect on a key realization: community engagement does not require grand gestures or scale; it often thrives on consistency and presence. Feeding the homeless, helping the elderly, or participating in neighborhood-building initiatives can all foster love when performed with intention and compassion. It is this essence of love that transforms an ordinary act into an extraordinary testament of faith in action.

Let us take inspiration from this journey and challenge ourselves to engage in service. Reflect on your own context, your community, and even what excites you. Where do your passions and skills align with the needs around you? Perhaps your strength lies in organizing events, connecting people, teaching, or simply listening. The possibilities are boundless, and all that matters is your willingness to take the first step.

The Seeker invites you to step forward and seek your place of love in action. Find opportunities that resonate with you, whether it's through supporting local nursing homes, volunteering at a children's hospital, or participating in ongoing community dialogues to promote social understanding. Dive deep into what your community truly needs and discover avenues of service that allow for authentic connections.

For many, the fear of inadequacy may linger, leaving thoughts like, "What difference can I really make?" Or perhaps there is concern about whether one has enough time or the necessary skills. Let us dismantle these barriers and embrace the truth that every small act of love is significant. The Seeker learned that genuine service is not measured by the size of the effort but by the depth of intent behind it. Engage not just physically, but emotionally, bring your whole self to the experience.

Consider creating a service group or forming a collective within your community. Invite friends or family to join you in your love in action. Whether it's through cooking community meals, organizing support for mental health initiatives, or collaborating with local charities, there is power in numbers. Together, you can tap into collective strengths, share resources, and build lasting memories that enrich your lives while serving others.

Additionally, you might explore the option of using social media as a platform for change. Initiate conversations, raise awareness for local needs, or rally volunteer support for causes close to your heart. It's a simple yet effective way to invite others into action, demonstrating that love and compassion can have a ripple effect in digital spaces.

Allow this chapter to culminate in a challenge: step into new territory filled with opportunities to serve. Whether you start small or dive headfirst into extended projects, remember that you are not alone. Community engagement is transformative, a way of showing up for one another as interconnected beings knitted together in love.

Embrace the discomfort that sometimes accompanies service. Perhaps volunteering in spaces that require challenging or difficult conversations may arise, especially in community programming that addresses societal issues. It's in these moments of tension that love is often most needed. An open heart and a willingness to learn can help steer you through the discomfort, challenging not only the status quo but also expanding your horizons and deepening your empathy.

Ultimately, the goal is not only to engage in action but to cultivate a spirit of love that extends beyond ourselves. Together, let us sow seeds of compassion, connection, and humility in our communities. Let us remember that life is richer when we generously give of our time, talents, and hearts, allowing ourselves to be a source of love and light for those around us.

In closing, the Seeker understands that living out love creates a powerful harmony. By serving others, he connects more deeply with his community and, in that service, draws closer to God. As we look beyond ourselves and our immediate circumstances, we realize that we are instruments of His love, called to engage and serve.

Now is the time to answer that call and step forward into the love that demands action. Let us reflect, engage, and live out the due intentions of community service, forging connections that birth beauty, hope, and love in every corner of our shared world.

Chapter 8:
The Power of Forgiveness

Forgiveness is an idea that often transcends the simple act of saying "I forgive you." It is a deep, emotional process that involves not just the relinquishment of anger or resentment, but its transformation into something profoundly nurturing: love. This subchapter aims to explore the intrinsic connection between love and forgiveness, shedding light on how God's love inspires us to forgive and how this divine mandate can graciously restore peace in our lives and relationships.

The journey toward true forgiveness is a reflection of the love that exists within us, waiting to be expressed and shared. It is equally a representation of the boundless love that God has for humanity. In the New Testament, the teachings of Jesus underscore the importance of forgiveness. In Matthew 6:14-15, Jesus states, "For if you forgive other people when they sin against you, your heavenly Father will also forgive you. But if you do not forgive others their sins, your Father will not forgive your sins." This powerful scripture illustrates the central role of forgiveness in the Christian faith and its vital connection to divine love and human relationships.

The concept of forgiveness is not merely a suggestion; it is portrayed as a divine mandate that reflects God's unconditional love for us. This love is demonstrated through Jesus' willingness to forgive even those who betrayed and crucified Him. Hanging on the cross, He uttered the words, "Father, forgive them, for they do not know what they are doing" (Luke 23:34). This supreme act of grace shows the highest form of God's love, the choice to forgive even when the pain feels unbearable. It teaches us that genuine forgiveness originates from the deepest wells of love, a love that calls us to rise above our hurts and live with greater compassion.

Personal stories of forgiveness can serve as poignant reminders of this powerful dynamic, illustrating the struggles and triumphs that people experience in the name of love. One such story features a woman named Martha, an individual who had carried the weight of resentment for many years due to her father's abandonment during her childhood. Martha's father chose to leave, pursuing a life that excluded his family. For years, she harbored anger and bitterness, which tainted her relationships with others, preventing her from experiencing love fully.

In the process of healing, Martha attended counseling, where she was confronted with the notion that her anger was not only hurting her father but was also holding her hostage. The counselor challenged her to consider forgiveness, suggesting that this act might help release the burden she had been carrying. At first, Martha struggled with the thought of forgiving someone who had hurt her so deeply. However, as she began to understand that forgiveness doesn't excuse what was done, it simply frees the one who was hurt, she began to feel a small spark of hope.

Through prayer and reflection, Martha sought God's help to cultivate compassion in her heart. She began journaling her thoughts and feelings, channeling her anger into words rather than allowing it to manifest in bitterness. It was during this time of introspection that she realized that forgiveness was an act of love, not just for her father, but for herself. It was a turning point when she recognized that holding onto resentment was detrimental to her mental and spiritual well-being.

Martha eventually reached out to her father, initiating a tentative conversation that led to understanding and empathy. In this moment of vulnerability, she expressed her hurt and disappointment but also her desire to forgive. To her surprise, her father expressed remorse and acknowledged the pain his actions had caused. That conversation became a catalyst for healing, leading to a gradual rebuilding of their relationship. Over time, they began to create new memories, grounded in a foundation of forgiveness and love.

This transformative experience reveals several fundamental aspects of forgiveness as an act of love. First, it showcases the importance of introspection and self-awareness in the forgiveness journey. Forgiveness cannot be forced; it must arise from a place of understanding and compassion. Martha's story serves as an inspiration to reflect on our own lives and the relationships that may require healing through forgiveness.

Moreover, Martha's journey highlights the critical role that divine love plays in the act of forgiveness. It was through seeking God's guidance that she was able to open her heart to the possibility of reconciliation. For many, including Martha, forgiving is closely linked with spiritual development, as it pushes us to face our faults, biases, and insecurities. We discover that love, even when hard to articulate, is what enables us to let go of our burdens and find a more peaceful life.

Another story that echoes the theme of forgiveness as an act of love involves a man named Derek, who experienced painful betrayal by a close friend. After years of camaraderie built on trust, Derek discovered that his friend had deceived him in a significant business deal, resulting in financial loss and emotional distress. Anger began to fester within Derek, leading him to question not only his friend's integrity but also the very foundation of their relationship.

At first, Derek responded defensively; he cut ties with his friend, believing that severing the relationship would protect him from further pain. However, the absence of friendship did not equate to healing. In his solitude, Derek realized that his bitterness was consuming him. He often found himself dwelling on the past, reliving the moments of betrayal in his mind, thus perpetuating his hurt. The realization struck him: clinging to resentment would never undo what had happened.

As Derek considered the possibility of forgiveness, he was faced with the challenge of overcoming his pride. This is often an underlying barrier to forgiveness that many encounter: the fear of appearing weak or vulnerable. Yet, as he engaged in a prayerful reflection, he began to understand that true strength lies not in holding onto grudges but in embodying love and grace.

After much contemplation and with encouragement from trusted friends, Derek decided to reach out to his former friend. The encounter was heart-wrenching; both men were anxious about the conversation ahead. However, in that moment of courage, Derek expressed his feelings of betrayal, but he also articulated his desire to forgive. To his surprise, his friend broke down in tears, expressing deep remorse for his actions and intoxicated by the burden of guilt for his betrayal.

This moment became a turning point for both Derek and his friend. Through tears, they began to rebuild their friendship, rooted in honesty and transparency. It was the act of forgiveness, the conscious choice to extend love despite pain, that allowed space for healing and renewal. For Derek, this experience reaffirmed the understanding that forgiveness is more than just a response; it is an ongoing journey. It transformed his outlook on relationships and solidified the truth that love, when truly expressed, has the power to heal and redeem.

As the Seeker navigates his own journey of forgiveness, he may encounter moments of hesitation and struggle. To forgive those who have hurt us deeply is not merely an act of goodwill; it is a formidable challenge rooted in vulnerability. The Seeker stands at a crossroads where the path of bitterness appears to promise reassurance against future pain, while the road to forgiveness beckons with the promise of healing.

As he thinks about his journey, the Seeker reflects on the example of Jesus, who showed the purest form of love. The act of giving oneself for the sake of others, even when faced with betrayal, is a powerful expression of God's love. As a follower of Christ, the Seeker must grapple with the teachings that demand he forgive, recognizing that love is perhaps the greatest teacher in the realm of forgiveness.

Yet, forgiveness does not occur in isolation; it involves deep engagement with oneself and the reality of relationships. The Seeker may find solace in the understanding that it is not uncommon to feel apprehensive about extending love to those who originally caused pain. To embrace the act of forgiveness as a revelation of love is a journey of self-discovery, an act of surrender and trust.

Moreover, the themes of struggle, doubt, and eventual triumph resonate throughout the realm of forgiveness. Consider the teachings found in Ephesians 4:32, which admonishes believers to "be kind to one another, tenderhearted, forgiving one another, as God in Christ forgave you." Such compelling words echo the call to embody love and grace, demonstrating how God extends forgiveness to us unconditionally.

As we reflect on these powerful narratives and teachings, it is crucial to recognize that forgiveness is a relational process. It involves both the act of letting go and the willingness to rebuild. Through understanding and compassion, the Seeker is encouraged to explore the emotional complexities of forgiveness, finding strength in vulnerability.

Reflective questions may help facilitate this personal exploration: Who do you struggle to forgive? How has holding onto resentment impacted your relationships? Are you aware of moments when love compelled you to forgive others? As the Seeker contemplates his responses, he becomes attuned to the intricacies of his own pain and hope, ultimately positioning himself to act with grace.

Ultimately, forgiveness is about restoring the soul and fostering a sense of peace within oneself. It is through the practice of forgiveness that we learn to embody the love of Christ, transcending our imperfections and embracing our humanity. Thus, as we journey through the landscape of forgiveness, we discover that acts of love possess the power to heal our wounds and restore essential connections.

May the Acts of forgiveness be a reflection of the love that binds humanity, a love that restores, nurtures, and essentially heals. Each story encapsulated within this subchapter serves as a reminder that, while the path of forgiveness may be challenging, it is equally filled with hope, grace, and the unwavering assurance that love always prevails. The Seeker's journey mirrors the collective human experience: a journey rooted in love, the essence of forgiveness and unyielding grace offered to us by a loving God.

The Process of Forgiving

Forgiveness is one of the most powerful acts of love and grace, yet it is often one of the most challenging journeys we embark upon. In a world rampant with misunderstandings, betrayals, and hurt, the call to forgive can feel disheartening. The weight of resentment can be heavy, and pride can build insurmountable walls around our hearts. However, embarking on the process of forgiveness opens the door to healing, not just for those we forgive, but also for ourselves. It creates space for reconciliation and restoration in our relationships with others and our relationship with God.

The journey of forgiveness is neither fast nor easy, but it is essential for our emotional and spiritual well-being. This subchapter will examine the steps involved in the forgiveness process, address common barriers such as pride and resentment, and outline practical steps to overcome these obstacles. In doing so, we will work alongside the Seeker as he navigates his unique journey toward forgiveness, guided by the wisdom of the Mentor.

As the Seeker sits in contemplation, the familiar and uncomfortable feelings of betrayal swell within him. Moments replay in his mind, conflicting emotions entangling his heart and soul. This is the critical first step: recognizing the need to forgive. The Seeker acknowledges that holding on to anger and resentment only deepens his pain and hinders his progress.

Acknowledging Hurt

The first step in the process of forgiveness is acknowledging our hurt. This may seem simple, but we often dismiss our feelings or try to rationalize them away. The Seeker recalls an incident of betrayal with a close friend, his heart heavy with unresolved pain. He remembers the words that stung and the promises that were broken. In the silence, the Mentor gently encourages the Seeker to articulate his feelings: "It's important to acknowledge the hurt for what it is. Denying your feelings only prolongs the healing process."

Recognizing and validating our pain allows us to confront it. We can start journaling about the event, expressing our anger, sadness, and confusion. This act of recognition sheds light on our experience, bringing it out of the shadows and allowing us to process it fully. Remember, it is not weakness to feel hurt, nor is it unspiritual; it is part of being human.

Reflective Exercise: Write down the details of the offense that hurt you. How did it make you feel? What emotions arise when you revisit that moment? Allow yourself to sit with these feelings without judgment.

Identifying Barriers

As the Seeker continues his journey, he must confront the barriers that hinder forgiveness. One of the most significant barriers is pride. Pride tells us that we are justified in our anger, that we should not be the ones to reach out or extend forgiveness. The Seeker contemplates his pride, reflecting on the reasons behind it. "If I forgive, does that mean I'm letting them off the hook?" he wonders aloud.

Pride can masquerade as self-righteousness, convincing us that we are on the moral high ground. However, the Mentor shares a crucial piece of wisdom: "Forgiveness is not about excusing the wrong. It's about freeing yourself from its grip." The Seeker begins to understand that forgiveness does not equate to condoning the behavior; rather, it is about choosing to release the offense and step toward healing.

Another barrier worth examining is resentment. Resentment is like a slow poison that eats the heart and mind. The Seeker struggles with bitterness, fighting against thoughts of revenge and payback. The Mentor asks, "What role does holding on to resentment play in your life? Is it protecting you or hindering you?"

As the Seeker reflects, he realizes that clinging to resentment only perpetuates his suffering. The act of forgiveness, although challenging, becomes an opportunity to reclaim personal power. The act of letting go can be incredibly liberating, a key that unlocks the door to a healthier, happier self.

Reflective Exercise: List the barriers you encounter in your own process of forgiveness. What emotions do they invoke? How have they shaped your perception of the individual who hurt you?

The Choice to Forgive

Having acknowledged his pain and identified barriers, the Seeker reaches the pivotal moment when he must choose to forgive. This is not a decision made lightly; it requires courage and vulnerability. The Mentor reinforces this choice by reminding the Seeker, "Forgiveness is a choice, not a feeling. You may not feel ready, but you can still choose to forgive."

The Seeker understands that forgiveness is an act of the will and not merely an emotional response. It involves surrendering the right to seek revenge or harbor resentment. He begins to envision what forgiveness could look like: an open hand instead of a clenched fist. It is helpful to imagine the person who hurt him bearing his struggles, flaws, and fears. This perspective shift can soften the heart and make it easier to empathize with the offender.

Reflective Exercise: Contemplate the choice to forgive. What does it mean for you personally? Who do you need to forgive, and why?

The Act of Forgiveness

Once the decision is made, the Seeker can take actionable steps towards forgiveness. One effective strategy is to pray for the person who has caused us pain. It may feel unnatural at first, but prayer can shift our perspective and soften our hearts. The Mentor advises, "Pray not for the hurt to be excused, but for peace and healing, for both you and the one who hurt you."

As the Seeker begins to pray, a sensation begins to stir within him. He is no longer praying from a place of bitterness but from a desire to seek healing. He discovers that prayer becomes a conduit for releasing his pain. With each prayer, the weight of his resentment lightens.

Another practical step is to communicate our forgiveness directly, if possible. It can be challenging and, at times, frightening to approach someone who has hurt us. The Seeker considers reaching out to the friend who betrayed him. He remembers the bond that once existed and wonders whether that bond can be revitalized through reconciliation. The Mentor encourages the Seeker to frame this conversation around his own healing rather than placing blame.

"Instead of saying, 'You hurt me,' try saying, 'I felt hurt by what happened between us,'" encourages the Mentor. This reframing promotes understanding and opens the door for a more productive conversation.

Reflective Exercise: Consider how you can express your forgiveness to the individual who hurt you. Would a conversation be an appropriate medium, or would a letter be more suitable for you?

Dealing with Ongoing Feelings

Forgiveness does not mean that feelings of hurt will vanish immediately. The Seeker acknowledges that unnecessary thoughts about the offense may continue to arise. This is where sustained effort and self-compassion play a crucial role. The Mentor offers a vital reminder: "Feelings are not inherently right or wrong; they are simply indicators of our emotional state."

When negative emotions resurface, the Seeker learns to acknowledge them without self-judgment. He reminds himself that healing is a journey, not a destination. When resentment rises again, the Seeker is reminded to make the choice once more, to forgive, again and again. Each time he does, it strengthens his decision and shows his dedication to healing.

The Mentor advises the Seeker to envision each act of forgiveness as a pebble thrown into a pond, creating ripples that extend outward. With every choice to forgive, he shapes his emotional landscape towards serenity and growth.

Reflective Exercise: When negative feelings emerge about the person you've forgiven, how will you address them? What strategies can you implement to remind yourself of your choice to forgive?

The Role of Community

Forgiveness is often a personal journey, but it can be significantly enriched by community support. The Seeker realizes that confiding in trusted friends or mentors can provide the encouragement needed to continue the process. Sharing our struggles with forgiveness highlights the shared human experience of pain and healing.

In community, we find strength and understanding; we hear stories that resonate with our own. The Mentor encourages the Seeker to seek guidance from those who have crossed this path before him. "Sharing your story can help you see the layers of your pain clearly and might even inspire others in their journeys toward forgiveness."

Moreover, surrounding ourselves with loving and supportive individuals who practice grace can create an environment that nurtures our heart's ability to forgive. The Seeker starts seeking opportunities to engage with others who are willing to cultivate an atmosphere of love and healing.

Reflective Exercise: Identify individuals in your life who can support you as you navigate forgiveness. How can you engage with them during this process?

Gratitude and Moving Forward

As the Seeker moves through the journey of forgiveness, something beautiful happens: he begins to feel free from the past and opens up to new joy. Each time he chooses to forgive, the heavy burden he carried grows lighter. No longer trapped by old failures, resentment, or pain, he is free to embrace life with a fresh start.

The Mentor reminds the Seeker to cultivate an attitude of gratitude towards life itself. By choosing to forgive, he invites joy, peace, and connection back into his heart. "Gratitude opens the door to grace, and grace magnifies love," the Mentor states.

Reflective Exercise: Take a moment to reflect on the newfound lightness you're feeling. What aspects of your life are you grateful for now that you have chosen to forgive? How has your perspective changed?

The journey toward forgiveness is undoubtedly challenging, marked by a myriad of emotions. Yet, within this process lies a remarkable opportunity for growth and transformation. The Seeker's journey shows an important truth about our relationship with both God and others: we are all imperfect and in need of grace. Just as God offers us unconditional love and forgiveness, so can we extend that same grace to others.

In this fabric of forgiveness, each thread woven together tells a story, our personal stories of hurt, struggle, healing, and ultimately liberation. As we traverse the winding road of forgiveness, may we remember the transformative power it holds, illuminating the way toward genuine connection and the unending love of God.

Stories of Redemption

It was a late, windy afternoon when Shana walked into the small coffee shop on the corner of the nearby Food Plaza. The sun was just lowering in the west as she took her usual place by the entrance. Her heart felt heavy, and as she wrapped her hands around her warm cup of coffee, she couldn't help but reflect on the weight of unhealed wounds from her past. Just weeks prior, she had taken the courageous step of reaching out to her estranged father, a man whose absence had loomed over her life like a dark cloud. Their relationship had been strained for years, festering with resentment and pain, a relationship marred by betrayal and misunderstanding.

Growing up, Shana had held a vivid image of a father who would cheer for her at her soccer games and sweep her off to dance, but her reality had been a stark contrast. Her father had chosen substances over family, leaving

Shana feeling abandoned and lost. After years of silence, fueled by anger, Shana found herself at a crossroads. She knew she had to confront the bitterness inside her, or it would continue to poison her heart and her relationships.

After sending a carefully crafted message asking to meet, she received a cautious response. They agreed to meet at the same coffee shop where Shana sat now, both nervous and unsure of what awaited them. As the door swung open and her father stepped inside, time seemed to stand still. His face was wrinkled, etched with lines that told tales of hardship and regret. In that moment, a small flicker of compassion ignited in Shana's heart. She realized that the man before her was not just the sum of his mistakes but also a soul in need of redemption.

The conversation that unfolded was a subtle interplay of emotions. They shared stories of their lives, filled with both quiet laughter and sorrowful silences. As they spoke, Shana discovered that her father had wrestled with his demons and was slowly emerging from the darkness of addiction. The journey of forgiveness was not easy, weighed down by tears, reminders of pain, and the long shadow of mistrust. Yet, as they exchanged their truths, the layers of hurt began to lift ever so slightly.

It was through this raw vulnerability that Shana found the strength to forgive her father. She realized that forgiveness was not about excusing the past but rather about releasing herself from its grip. She learned to see her father as a flawed human being, one who had fallen but deserved a chance to rise again. Their reconciliation did not magically repair years of damage, nor did it erase the scars they both carried. However, it marked a new beginning, a path paved with compassion, healing, and understanding.

In sharing her story of redemption, Shana hopes to inspire others grappling with similar battles in their relationships. Forgiveness is a complex and often messy process, but it is also immensely powerful. It opens doors that were once tightly sealed shut and allows love to seep back into fractured lives.

Another powerful story emerged from James, a middle-aged man whose life spiraled out of control following the loss of his wife. Overwhelmed by grief, he let bitterness take over, pushing away friends and family who only wished to help him. His anger built up like a volcano waiting to erupt, and it did, one fateful night, leading to a confrontation with his dear friend Mark. After a heated exchange filled with accusations and harsh words, their friendship ended abruptly.

Months passed, and while James struggled to cope, he often reflected on their last conversation. As the glow of the holiday season approached, he recalled the warmth of their friendship, the laughter they shared, the late-night chats, a stark contrast to the weight of solitude he now carried. It was during one of these moments of reflection that James recognized the need to forgive himself for his past actions and approach Mark in an attempt to heal what had been broken.

The next day, James mustered the courage to reach out, crafting a message filled with a heartfelt apology. The response was cautious but hopeful. They agreed to meet after a long silence, and when their eyes met for the first time since that ill-fated night, James felt the weight of regret pressing heavily upon him.

The conversation that unfolded was weighed down with emotions, from the tension of unspoken words to the vulnerability of shared sorrow. It was not easy, but as James opened up about his grief and the pain he had caused, he saw the flicker of understanding in Mark's eyes. They both shared tears, a mixture of healing and heartache, as they began the process of rebuilding their friendship.

Through this experience, James found that forgiveness was not an endpoint but a journey, a winding road filled with detours. He discovered the importance of patience and grace, both for himself and for others. Their friendship, once fractured, began to mend slowly, fortified with deeper respect and understanding. The bond that had been tested by pain emerged stronger than before, proving that redemption was possible through the power of forgiveness.

One of the most profound stories of redemption comes from Anna, a woman who carried the burden of a betrayal that shattered her family. After discovering her husband's infidelity, she felt like her world had crumbled. The emotions were overwhelming: betrayal, anger, and despair raged within her, turning her home into a battlefield filled with broken trust.

Initially, Anna's heart was locked tight against any semblance of forgiveness. She thought, "How could I forgive someone who shattered my life?" Yet, as the days turned into months, she began to realize that holding onto that anger was only hurting her. She saw a therapist who guided her through the process of grief and helped her understand the essence of forgiveness, not just for her husband, but for herself.

After seeking professional help and finding solace in her faith community, Anna decided to confront her husband. They sat together, and as he confessed the depth of his wrongdoings, truly understanding the pain he had inflicted, Anna felt a shift within her. It was through his genuine remorse and commitment to change that Anna began to rediscover love, not just for him, but for herself as well.

Forgiving him was not instantaneous; it was a gradual process. Together, they embarked on a journey to rebuild their relationship, which involved setting healthy boundaries and seeking a deeper understanding of one another. Anna learned to communicate her feelings without blame, and in doing so, she unexpectedly found that she had not only forgiven her husband but also allowed herself to heal.

Today, Anna shares her story of redemption, emphasizing that forgiveness does not imply forgetting or tolerating hurtful behavior. Instead, it is about reclaiming your power and finding the peace that lies within. Her story serves as a beacon for those who find themselves in similar situations, reminding them that healing is not only possible but also essential.

Each of these stories underscores the profound truth that forgiveness is intertwined with love and the potential for redemption. These individuals all faced different circumstances, but at their core was the same fundamental struggle: the desire for healing and connection. In a world where relationships can often go awry, these narratives remind us of the remarkable capacity for restoration that resides within forgiveness.

As we reflect on these stories, we are prompted to consider our own journeys, moments in our lives when we have struggled with forgiveness or have sought to be forgiven. Perhaps we are burdened by unresolved conflicts or bitter grudges that keep us trapped. The path to healing may seem overwhelming, but it begins with a single step - a choice to show grace to ourselves and others. In moments of contemplation, consider the following questions:

1. Have you experienced a situation where forgiveness transformed your relationship? What steps did you take to reach that point?

2. Are there relationships in your life that could benefit from the healing power of forgiveness? What might that process look like for you?

3. Have you found it challenging to forgive yourself for past mistakes or missteps? How can you begin to show yourself the same grace you would extend to others?

4. In what ways can you invite the spirit of forgiveness into your daily life, fostering a culture of grace and understanding within your community?

5. Reflect on the power of love. How has love played a role in your willingness to forgive or seek forgiveness?

Ultimately, the stories of redemption offer more than just testimonials; they provide profound insights into the essence of forgiveness. They remind us that love is an ongoing journey marked by the courage to confront pain and to seek reconciliation. Each act of forgiveness has the potential to alter the path of our lives, leading us toward profound healing and the restoration of relationships. As we navigate our own stories, let us embrace the transformative power of forgiveness, allowing it to guide us toward a future filled with hope and love.

Chapter 9:
Building A Love-Filled Community

The Importance of Community in Love

In our fast-paced, often fragmented world, the search for authentic, meaningful connections can feel more elusive than ever. Yet, within the heart of the Christian faith lies a powerful truth: we are designed for community. Community isn't just about spending time with others; it's about building love, offering support, and helping one another grow in understanding God's endless love.

As we explore this vital role of community in fostering love, we will reflect on biblical teachings about fellowship and unity, drawing wisdom from both scripture and the lived experiences of individuals navigating their own community journeys. The Seeker, a relatable character in this narrative, represents the struggles and triumphs many of us face as we seek meaningful relationships. We will accompany him on his journey to build connections that mirror the unconditional love of God, emphasizing the transformation that can occur when we engage in community.

In the beginning, God created humanity not as isolated beings, but as beings meant to exist in relationship. Genesis tells us that it was not good for man to be alone (Genesis 2:18). This foundational truth echoes throughout scripture, reinforcing the idea that we are called to share our lives, not just with God but with one another.

Picture the early church, as described in Acts 2:42-47. This community was characterized by deep fellowship, generous sharing, and unwavering commitment to one another. The believers devoted themselves to the apostles' teaching, and to fellowship, to the breaking of bread and prayer. Amazing miracles were performed through the apostles, and the community flourished. People were drawn to this expression of love, their hearts opened, and their spirits grew stronger through the power of unity.

This image of the early church serves as a blueprint for nurturing love within a community. The joy of shared meals, the bonds formed through common faith, and the support offered during trials illustrate the beauty of living in community. We are reminded that when we choose to engage with one another, we are better equipped to reflect God's love and support each other's spiritual and emotional growth.

The Seeker, when first introduced to the idea of community, felt a mix of hesitation and hope. He had spent years feeling isolated, struggling with the fear of rejection and vulnerability. Yet there was a spark of yearning within him, a deep desire to belong, to be known, and to be loved. He started attending a local church, unsure of what to expect. The vibrant energy of the community welcomed him, and he quickly found himself embraced in an environment rich with love and acceptance.

As the Seeker began to immerse himself in this newfound community, he was struck by the diversity present among the members. Young and old, single and married, people across various backgrounds gathered to worship together. He witnessed the richness that this diversity brought to the understanding and practice of love. Conversations flowed freely as individuals shared their struggles and triumphs, offering both empathy and encouragement.

Through potluck dinners and prayer groups, the Seeker discovered the ways in which community nurtures love. One evening, he joined a small group that gathered weekly, intentionally creating a space for vulnerability and connection. It was here he learned that sharing his challenges did not make him weak but, rather, opened the door for deeper relationships. By expressing his own vulnerabilities, he also created an open atmosphere for others to share. This mutual exchange of experiences strengthened his bonds, allowing for God's love to flow freely toward him.

The Seeker experienced firsthand how community can amplify one's understanding of love. Each member offered unique perspectives, prompting him to reflect on his definitions of love and his roles within the community. He often remembered a particular evening when a member confided in the group about an ongoing personal struggle. As the group sat in a sacred silence, offering support through prayer, he realized how love manifests through tangible acts of kindness, understanding, and genuine concern for one another.

These moments illuminated a vital truth: love is not merely an emotion; it is an action. The teachings of Jesus echo this principle as he commands his followers to love one another as he has loved them (John 13:34). Within the embrace of community, the Seeker found that love could be expressed through service, whether it was helping a neighbor, participating in outreach efforts, or simply being present with someone in their suffering.

Furthermore, the Seeker observed how the collective faith of the community served as a catalyst for encouraging one another in their spiritual journeys. The sharing of testimonies became a powerful tool for growth. As individuals recounted experiences of God's faithfulness, others found renewed hope in their own struggles. This cycle of sharing and supporting reflected the biblical promise that we are stronger together. Ecclesiastes 4:9-10 reminds us that "two are better than one, because they have a good return for their labor: If either of them falls down, one can help the other up." In community, we find the strength, encouragement, and motivation to continue pursuing love and faithfulness during difficult times.

Yet, the Seeker also encountered challenges within his community. Every relationship has its complexities; misunderstandings can arise, and conflicts may emerge. There were times when the Seeker felt disheartened by gossip or judgment among members. This experience led to a deeper introspection about the nature of love, grace, and forgiveness. He realized that nurturing an environment of love takes intention and effort.

The Seeker learned the importance of empathy and humility, recognizing that no one is perfect and that everyone is on their own journey of growth. The wisdom shared by the Mentor, a wise and gentle figure in his life, reminded him, "Community is like a garden; it requires tending. The weeds of discord can choke out love if left unchecked, but kindness, forgiveness, and communication can cultivate an environment where love flourishes." With the Mentor's guidance, the Seeker grew more adept at navigating tensions, remaining committed to reconciliation and fostering unity.

As the Seeker continued to explore his community's dynamics, he began to envision how he could serve as a catalyst for positive change. He felt God's calling to become an agent of love within his sphere of influence.

Inspired by the biblical call to hospitality, he opened his home for small group gatherings, creating space for everyone to feel valued and seen.

He began to organize community service projects, inviting others to join in as they addressed local needs. As they demonstrated love through practical actions, they witnessed a ripple effect. Neighbors who once barely acknowledged one another began to engage, fostering deeper connections that extended beyond the church walls. In these moments, the Seeker experienced the profound impact that a community rooted in love can have on individuals and those around them.

The Seeker also felt called to find new ways to make everyone feel included. He began talking with people from different backgrounds, hoping to learn from their stories and understand their points of view. Through these dialogues, he recognized that every individual brings unique gifts and experiences that enrich the community and its expression of love.

The importance of inclusivity cannot be understated. A community that embraces diversity cultivates a richer understanding of God's love. It reflects the beauty of God's creation, where each piece contributes to the overall beauty and unity of the body of Christ. The Seeker learned to appreciate different cultures and saw the worth in every person's voice, building a space where love could grow without limits.

As the Seeker navigated these experiences, he also faced personal challenges. The pressures of balancing work, family, and community involvement weighed heavily on him. There were moments of doubt and exhaustion, where he wondered if his efforts were truly making a difference. During one particularly challenging week, he reached out to his small group for support. The outpouring of encouragement, prayers, and offers to help refueled his spirit. This experience underscored the vital role that community plays in fortifying individuals during life's challenging moments.

The scripture in Galatians 6:2 instructs us to "carry each other's burdens, and in this way, you will fulfill the law of Christ." The Seeker witnessed the beauty of this call materialize through acts of love, as his community rallied around one another in times of need. The gift of companionship during trials brought comfort, reminding him of the perfect love of Christ, which is embodied in community support.

Reflecting on these experiences, the Seeker became increasingly aware of his own role in contributing to a love-filled community. He felt empowered to foster authenticity and connection, recognizing that creating a supportive environment requires intentional vulnerability. In sharing his own struggles and victories, he invited others to do the same, reinforcing the notion that community is a safe space for resilience and growth.

As we consider our own communities, we are called to examine how we can contribute to creating love-filled environments. What strengths do we bring to the table? How can we use our unique experiences to nurture relationships? These reflective questions invite us to engage actively in our communities, fostering a spirit of love and support.

Perhaps we are called to initiate conversations with those who may feel marginalized. It could be as simple as inviting someone to share a meal or lending a listening ear to a friend experiencing hardship. In doing so, we mirror the unconditional love of God, affirming that each person is worthy of care and belonging.

Additionally, we must reflect on how we can cultivate inclusivity in our communities. Are there individuals who feel left out? What can we do to create safe spaces where everyone feels welcome to contribute their story? As we become aware of subtle barriers that may exist, we empower ourselves to act with love and grace, ultimately fostering unity and fellowship.

Furthermore, we should recognize the importance of mutual support. Community is about being there for one another, not just in times of celebration but also during moments of pain and struggle. This reciprocal nature encourages growth, strengthens relationships, and embodies God's love in a profound way.

In embracing the importance of community, we discover that we are not merely passive participants but active agents of love in our own stories and those around us. The Seeker's journey illustrates that true fulfillment is found not in isolation but in relationships grounded in the love of Christ.

Amid division and disconnection, we are called to be beacons of light, drawing on the rich teachings of our faith to build communities that reflect God's heart. Let us hold fast to the knowledge that love, nurtured within our community, can transform lives, heal wounds, and provide the foundation for spiritual growth.

As we conclude this exploration into the vital role of community in nurturing love, may we be reminded that our engagement matters. Each act of kindness, each moment of connection, resonates far beyond what we can see. Together, we can create a love-filled community that bears witness to the radical, unconditional love of God, ultimately drawing others into the deeper truth of belonging and acceptance.

In every potluck, prayer gathering, or shared moment, let us commit to embodying love that celebrates our differences while uniting us in our common purpose. Through our shared experiences, we create an environment where everyone is seen, valued, and loved, reflecting beautifully the heart of God in a world that desperately needs it.

Creating Inclusive Spaces

Creating inclusive spaces is one of the most tangible expressions of God's love in community life. As we explore what inclusivity truly means, we see that building a welcoming and loving community takes purpose, compassion, and a genuine respect for diversity. God's love knows no boundaries, extending to every individual, regardless of their background, beliefs, or struggles. Within a society divided by differences, the call to embrace inclusivity can reshape lives and build communities that reveal the heart of our Creator.

The importance of inclusivity cannot be overstated. It invites people into a sense of belonging, affirming their worth and value in an environment that may often push them to the margins. When individuals feel accepted, they can begin to flourish and contribute their unique gifts to the communal tapestry, enriching the lives of those around them. Inclusivity allows us to move beyond mere tolerance; it invites us to celebrate diversity, cultivate understanding, and foster a genuine sense of community where every voice is heard and every story matters.

As we consider what it means to create inclusive spaces, let us reflect on the experiences of those who have walked this path. One such story comes from a woman named Amy, who felt marginalized in her church community due to her background. Raised in a single-parent household, Amy often felt different from her peers, who came from more traditional family structures. While attending church services, she sat quietly in the back, grappling with feelings of unworthiness and isolation.

However, everything changed when a small group of church members, known as the "Welcome Team," took it upon themselves to reach out. They offered Amy a warm invitation to join their activities, creating spaces where individuals from various backgrounds could come together to share their experiences and faith. This simple act of kindness sparked a transformation; Amy felt seen, heard, and valued. She soon became an active member of the community, using her own experiences to encourage others who might feel similarly alone.

Amy's story is a testament to how intentional efforts can create spaces of acceptance and love. Inclusivity calls us to recognize and remove barriers that prevent individuals from participating fully in community life. These barriers can be physical, emotional, or social. As we strive to create inclusive environments, we must examine our surroundings, the way our spaces are structured, how we communicate, and the policies we implement. Are our signs welcoming? Do we offer resources for those with disabilities? Are programming schedules considerate of varied life circumstances? By being mindful of these factors, we can collectively cultivate a more inclusive community.

The Mentor in this journey reminds us that inclusivity begins with that all-important first step: acknowledging and embracing our own biases and preconceptions. It requires a willingness to listen and learn from others, particularly those whose experiences differ from our own. It is easy to remain in our comfort zones, but true inclusivity invites us to step outside of them. By opening our hearts and minds, we can begin to form deeper connections that transcend differences and foster unity.

One powerful example of an inclusive space in action is a community center called "Unity Hall." Unity Hall was developed with the mission of creating an environment where people from all walks of life could come together to learn, grow, and connect. The founders recognized that uniting people requires more than merely providing a physical space; it requires cultivating a culture of openness and acceptance.

At Unity Hall, diversity is not just tolerated, it is celebrated. Regular events showcase cultural heritage, encouraging individuals to share their stories, traditions, and talents. The community hosts music nights, cooking classes, and art workshops, each designed to highlight diverse backgrounds while promoting understanding and appreciation for one another. It is within these shared experiences that bonds are formed, and individuals discover the common threads that weave them together, regardless of their differences.

The Mentor, drawing from the example of Unity Hall, encourages readers to consider how they can actively cultivate inclusive spaces within their own communities. One way to do this is by creating forums for dialogue. Inviting diverse voices to share their experiences fosters understanding and empathy, breaking down walls of misunderstanding and fear. These discussions can take place in various formats, such as community forums, small groups, or workshops.

Alongside dialogue, the Mentor emphasizes the significance of accessibility. Inclusivity is not just about welcoming individuals into established structures; it is about ensuring that everyone can engage in the community at every level. This means being aware of physical accessibility, but it also extends to emotional and social aspects. Creating a culture of acceptance means that individuals who may have felt excluded in the past are encouraged to actively participate without fear of judgment or rejection.

Our collective experiences often highlight the need for various support systems within our communities. For instance, mentorship programs can be an effective way to foster inclusivity and belonging. These programs can pair individuals from different backgrounds and experiences, allowing them to learn from one another while offering guidance and support. As these relationships develop, they create spaces for vulnerability, authenticity, and growth. It is a reciprocal arrangement that ultimately strengthens the collective fabric of the community.

Reflections on inclusivity encourage us to evaluate our own circles closely. Do we surround ourselves with diverse perspectives? Are we open to engaging with those whose experiences differ from our own? Asking these questions can illuminate areas where we may unknowingly perpetuate exclusivity. The Mentor suggests creating a personal action plan: identify at least one individual from a different background and reach out to them. Share a meal or conversation. Listen to their stories. Understand their aspirations, fears, and triumphs. This simple action can bridge gaps that have long existed and pave the way for a deeper sense of community.

Inclusivity also invites us to challenge stereotypes and take a stand against discrimination. The Mentor recalls the story of a high school student named Jacob, who witnessed bullying targeting a classmate because of their sexual orientation. Motivated by a sense of justice, Jacob decided to speak up, even when it was uncomfortable. With a sincere desire to reflect Christ's love, he encouraged his friends to treat everyone, including their LGBTQ+ peers, with kindness and respect. Rather than focusing on differences, Jacob helped create opportunities for open conversations that promoted understanding and compassion. His courage helped foster a spirit of dignity and care throughout the school.

Stories like Jacob's show that true inclusivity takes courage, the courage to speak up for those who feel unheard, to stand for what is right, and to open ourselves with honesty and vulnerability. When we acknowledge that we each have a role to play in fostering inclusivity, we create collective movements capable of enacting real change.

To inspire further reflection, the Mentor encourages readers to engage in questions about their own communities and personal interactions:

1. Who in your life feels excluded or marginalized? What practical steps can you take to reach out and create a welcoming environment for them?

2. When have you felt excluded? What emotions and thoughts arose during that experience? How can this understanding guide your actions toward inclusivity?

3. Reflect on a time when you felt empowered to make a difference in your community. How can you apply that same enthusiasm to champion inclusivity today?

4. In what ways can your community cultivate inclusivity through events or activities that celebrate diversity? What ideas come to mind that you could propose to your local leaders or organize yourself?

5. Consider your current social circles. Are there ways you can broaden your engagements to intentionally include diverse perspectives?

By taking the time to reflect on these prompts, we can illuminate paths toward inclusivity both personally and communally. Creating spaces of acceptance and love requires consistent effort, shared leadership, and a genuine desire to uplift those around us.

In our journey toward establishing inclusive environments, let us remember the importance of patience and grace. Change takes time, and fostering inclusivity may come with its own set of challenges. Yet, every small step taken in love contributes to a greater vision of unity.

Further, the Mentor encourages readers to gather feedback from their communities on perceived inclusivity. Conduct surveys or discussions that invite honest reflections on how valued individuals feel in various spaces. This soul-searching reveals how effectively we are living out our commitment to inclusivity and highlights areas where growth is still needed.

With every effort, we can inspire others to take part in creating a culture of love and acceptance. In schools, workplaces, and social circles, a ripple effect occurs when one individual stands up for inclusivity. We pave the way for others to do the same.

As we conclude this discussion, let us celebrate the beauty of diversity in our communities and honor the narratives that constitute our shared human experience. Each person carries a spark of God's love within them, waiting to be seen and accepted. The real challenge isn't noticing how we differ, but learning to embrace what we share as humans, building connections that have the power to change the world around us.

Building inclusive spaces is an essential expression of God's boundless love, a love that sees potential where others may see division. It is our responsibility to answer the call to love boldly and inclusively, reflecting the heart of the Creator in every interaction we share. Together, let us invite others into spaces of acceptance, embodying the love that welcomes all.

Serving Together in Love

As the first rays of morning sunlight streamed across the bustling neighborhood, the air buzzed with excitement and anticipation. In a small park at the heart of the community, a vibrant blend of colors emerged as families, friends, and neighbors gathered for the annual Community Love Day. This event was not just a celebration; it was an embodiment of what it meant to serve together in love.

Throughout the park, booths were set up, each representing a different service initiative. Children painted banners promoting kindness, while teenagers organized a food drive for local charities. Elderly community members shared stories of their past volunteer experiences, inspiring younger generations with tales of hope and resilience. This day had become a tradition, a day devoted to demonstrating love in tangible ways, a day that transformed the ordinary into extraordinary through the power of collective action.

For Ellen, a devoted member of the community, this day held a special significance. As a Seeker on her journey to understand love, she recalled her first experience with community service. Fresh out of college and feeling lost, Ellen came across a flyer for a local food pantry seeking volunteers. Curious but unsure, she decided to attend. That decision marked the turning point in her life, leading her to discover the life-changing impact of serving alongside others.

As she mingled with fellow community members, Ellen felt a renewed sense of purpose. The connections formed through shared work amplified her understanding of love. She remembered how, during her first day at the food pantry, she met David, a single father struggling to provide for his two young children. His story resonated with her, but more than that, the support and compassion she witnessed from other volunteers moved her immensely. Together, they worked tirelessly, assembling food parcels not just as a task, but as an act of love that met real needs.

The concept of community service was one that transcended the act itself; it embodied a collective heart, united in purpose. As Ellen led a group of volunteers that day, she knew they were not just distributing food; they were extending love, creating bonds, and offering hope. The joy of working together fostered a sense of belonging, a shared commitment not just to meet physical needs but to nurture souls.

Building a love-filled community often begins with recognizing the significance of shared action. When individuals come together with a common purpose, they not only address immediate needs but also cultivate a deeper understanding of each other. Conversations flow more freely among people who are actively engaged in service, forming connections that might not otherwise happen. Ellen reminisced about her initial hesitations: fears of inadequacy left her as she shared her heart with others, learning and growing in the process.

The power of shared stories cannot be underestimated. The shared experience of serving opens a doorway to understanding perspectives that one might never confront alone. As Ellen took part in more community activities, she began to see that everyone she met had their own story, each one filled with challenges, victories, and hopes, all connected through their shared efforts. Each project became an opportunity to witness the beauty of diversity in purpose and the oneness found in love.

Community Love Day culminated in a powerful moment, as Ellen stood at the front of the crowd, her voice resonating with the passion she felt. "Love isn't just a feeling; it's an action," she declared. "Today, we've shown that when we serve together, we are not only making a difference, we are embodying God's love. Every act of kindness amplifies the love we share; it reinforces our bonds as a community and transforms lives. Together, we are stronger!"

Inspired by her words, attendees began to share their own stories of love in service. John, a retired veteran who had dedicated his life to supporting local youth, spoke passionately about a mentorship program he initiated. "I remember the first group of kids who joined us," he shared. "Many came from tough backgrounds, but through shared experiences, whether it was tutoring, sports, or crafts, we created a family. Together, we learned resilience, hope, and love." His words, echoing through the crowd, resounded the transformative nature of building relationships through service.

Sophia, a single mother, stood next to him, sharing how volunteering had brought her more than just a sense of purpose. "When I enrolled my kids in the after-school program that John runs, they not only received support in their studies, but they flourished as individuals. I found a community of love where I felt seen and valued, even in my struggles." As she spoke, others nodded in agreement, feeling the weight of her words.

Each narrative intermingled like the laughter and chatter filling the park. A renewed hope sparked in the hearts of those present, an understanding that love grows exponentially when shared among a community. They envisioned projects that might extend beyond the day, ideas blossoming for future initiatives that could address various needs. From organizing food drives to advocating for mental health resources, everyone felt a fresh commitment to serve with fervor, not just during special events, but as a lifestyle.

As the evening unfolded, Ellen caught sight of an elderly couple sitting quietly on a bench, their expressions reflecting both warmth and sadness. Instinctively, she felt drawn to them, curious about their story. "Hi! How's your day going?" she asked, kneeling beside them. They shared their experiences of volunteering in their younger days, reminiscing about how they once led a community garden initiative. "It brought people together, united by a love for nature and nourishment," the husband said, his eyes lighting up.

"Why don't you join us again?" Ellen proposed. "There are so many ways you could inspire others with your knowledge and experience." Just like that, Ellen saw another bond forming in their community, a new connection where wisdom could be shared from one generation to the next.

This day, full of exchange and commitment, was not merely about the act of service—it was a testament to love flourishing in action. As the event concluded, Ellen felt ignited with a sense of urgency. This was not just an isolated day; it was an invitation to participate in God's love on a broader scale. She understood that building a love-filled community was a continuous journey, one where love is reflected not just in words, but more importantly, in deeds.

In the weeks that followed, the spirit of community grew beyond the park. Feeling inspired, Ellen began organizing small gatherings, not just planned events, but warm spaces where people could talk, share, and grow together. These evenings turned into potlucks, sharing meals around tables where laughter mingled with shared stories. Neighbors began to talk about their passions, hobbies, dreams, and visions for a more connected community.

Jeremy, an artist in the neighborhood, suggested a painting project celebrating the essence of community. Collaboratively, they painted not just walls, but the essence of love through vibrant colors and shared messages. Each stroke of the brush became a symbol of their commitment to nurture a space where everyone felt seen and valued.

Through these engagements, Ellen learned firsthand that even the smallest gesture could lead to monumental change. Offering a helping hand, creating a listening ear, or simply sharing a meal with someone facing challenges contributed to a rich tapestry of support that reflected God's love in action. It was a tangible example of how, when we work together, love multiplies and deepens.

However, they also faced hurdles along the way. Not every initiative was successful, and not every gathering was well-attended. But they learned that love is not always about results; sometimes it is found in the attempt, in the heart behind the action. When a few volunteers showed up at the community garden, feeling disheartened, they realized they had each other. They shared laughs over weeds pulled and seedlings planted, feeding off each other's passion, and that camaraderie proved to be an invaluable experience, perhaps even more than finishing the garden itself.

Ellen knew that building a love-filled community required resilience and commitment from everyone involved. Even in these unsettled times marked by division and hurriedness, taking intentional steps to unite their hearts in love was a divine calling. Encouraged by countless stories of love in action, the community flourished as it continued to explore new avenues for service.

As the months passed, the love that had bloomed in the park now prospered throughout their community. Individuals began to notice needs that might have gone unseen before, offering support to families impacted by job loss, organizing clothing drives for the less fortunate, and launching an after-school tutoring program for children struggling in school.

In one notable instance, a man named Mark reached out to Ellen after witnessing her passion for service. He shared his heart for those facing homelessness and proposed a community cookout and clothing drive. "I want to welcome our neighbors in need, to show them compassion," he enthused. Together, they rallied more community members to pitch in, cooking, collecting clothing, and creating inviting spaces to share meals, foster conversations, and address immediate needs.

As the event unfolded, those once considered "the other" became beloved friends. Relationships blossomed in those few hours as people shared not only meals but stories, laughter, and mutual respect. Underneath the sunlit skies, love radiated brightly.

Through such experiences, Ellen discovered that every act of service creates ripples of love extending far beyond what the eye can see. Each individual felt the impact, creating connections with others and inspiring more acts of kindness. Stories of redemption emanating from their service reached neighboring communities, demonstrating that love knows no boundaries.

Ultimately, serving together in love not only transformed those they sought to help; it also transformed the hearts of those who engaged in service. Through her journey, Ellen discovered that giving has the power to heal both the giver and the community. She realized that love, when shared, spreads like a beautiful melody, bringing people together and creating unity in their diversity.

As they continued to grow as a community, Ellen felt a profound sense of responsibility to carry this lesson forward. She began to organize regular meetings to discuss new projects, sharing the successes and failures of their collective journey. Emphasizing that everyone had something unique to offer, she encouraged openness in contribution, underscoring that every voice mattered in crafting a love-filled atmosphere.

In conclusion, as each community member returned to their daily lives after Community Love Day, the spirit of service continued to linger, a reminder that love should be an ongoing practice, rooted deeply in honoring each other's stories and needs. The call-to-action rings clearer than ever: We are called to participate in the great work of love, to dedicate ourselves to building and nurturing communities where kindness flows freely.

Love is amplified when shared collectively; it ignites a fire within us all, a purpose that transcends ordinary days, binds us together, and reflects the divine love that chases us down, fights 'til we're found, and rejoices in every act of kindness we share.

May we challenge ourselves to engage in our communities, to listen, to learn, to share, to serve, and, in doing so, embody the very essence and love of God. Together, we can create a love-filled community reflecting God's endless, boundless love, a community that inspires hope and nurtures every heart. As we embrace this calling, let us carry forward the love lit within us, spreading it far and wide, knowing that when we serve together, we serve not just our neighbors but God Himself.

Chapter 10:
Eternal Love

The Promise of Everlasting Love

The sun set below the horizon, painting the sky in shades of orange and purple. The Seeker stood by a quiet lake, admiring the beauty reflected in the water. In that peaceful moment, as the cool breeze wrapped around him, he thought about the kind of love that endures through time, struggles, and change. Then a clear thought came to him, one he was only now beginning to understand, the promise of God's everlasting love.

"Everlasting love," he whispered to himself, letting the phrase roll off his tongue like a prayer. Those two words carried weight, encapsulating an assurance that he had been yearning for. This love was not fleeting; it was not contingent on his actions, his successes, or even his failures. It was steadfast, unwavering, and most importantly, eternal. Perhaps it was time to revisit the foundational truths he had learned about this divine love, to reflect on how such a promise could provide comfort during life's inevitable storms.

As he searched within, a medley of moments flowed through his mind. Memories of despair and heartache, mixed with glimmers of hope, flooded his consciousness like waves crashing upon the shore. Many times, he had faced challenges that seemed insurmountable. The burden of loss, the isolation of depression, the whirlwind of uncertainty, each had cast shadows over his spirit. Yet, even in those darkest moments, there had been an unexplainable presence, a gentle whisper reminding him that he was loved. The Seeker began to realize that the essence of God's love could be traced not only in his feelings but also in scriptural affirmations that echoed through history.

He recalled the letter the Apostle Paul wrote to the Romans: "For I am convinced that neither death nor life, neither angels nor demons, neither the present nor the future, nor any powers, neither height nor depth, nor anything else in all creation, will be able to separate us from the love of God that is in Christ Jesus our Lord" (Romans 8:38-39, NIV). The words leaped from the page and pierced his heart. Nothing, absolutely nothing, could sever the connection that he had with the Creator. In times of turmoil, he had let himself be swayed by the storms of doubt, but now, standing at the water's edge, he felt anchored by the knowledge that God's love was tenacious.

The Seeker thought of the trials endured by biblical figures, those who had walked the earth before him, facing struggles that seemed to dwarf his own. Take Job, for instance. His story of losing everything yet still proclaiming, "Though He slay me, yet will I hope in Him" (Job 13:15, NIV), stood as a testament to unwavering faith in divine love that transcended circumstance. Job's posture towards God's love amid his suffering became a light in the darkness for the Seeker, revealing a perspective he longed to adopt.

He remembered his own hardships: the pain of a fractured relationship, the anguish of losing a beloved family member, and the relentless pressure of societal expectations. During those seasons, he often questioned his worthiness to receive love, particularly God's love. Yet, through each layer of despair, God's grace persisted, encouraging him to lean into this promise of eternal love. The weight of his struggles didn't diminish God's desire to embrace him; rather, it magnified the depth of that embrace when he finally surrendered.

This realization made him reflect on the meaning of true freedom, the freedom to receive love without conditions. He understood that God's love isn't a reward for good behavior or a result of personal success. Instead, it was a gift freely given. A passage from 1 John surfaced in his heart: "See what great love the Father has lavished on us, that we should be called children of God! And that is what we are!" (1 John 3:1, NIV). To be called a child of God illustrated the intimacy and permanence of this relationship. In the light of that love, he found solace, recognizing that he didn't have to earn his sonship. The truth of being cherished by God was a steady song, resonating through the chaos of life.

The Seeker's reflections deepened as he sat upon a bench overlooking the tranquil waters. He had witnessed the fleeting nature of human affection, how love can shift with circumstances—conditional, and at times, selfish.

But the love of God? It remained constant, grounding him amidst turbulent waters. The Psalms echoed in his soul—"His love endures forever" (Psalm 136:1, NIV), and the meaning of those simple words unfolded delicately, like the petals of a blooming flower. This love was not only eternal but also transformative, reshaping the narrative of his life story into one of hope.

He thought about all the times he had tried to control situations or protect himself from being hurt, driven by fear of judgment or rejection. But as he grew deeper in faith, he began to understand that real love requires vulnerability. There was wisdom in the age-old adage that love's essence flourishes when shared openly, without pretense. With each act of love he encountered, whether from a stranger's kind smile or a friend's support during trying times, the Seeker began to grasp that love, when reciprocated, became a radiant light piercing through the murky doubts that occasionally clouded his mind.

The Seeker thought about the nature of hope in the context of God's love—how, even in despair, hope could be birthed from a deep understanding of the divine promise. In times of hardship, he had often sought solace in scriptural truths, affirmations of God's faithfulness during trials. The words of Lamentations 3:22-23 rang true: "The steadfast love of the Lord never ceases; His mercies never come to an end; they are new every morning; great is Your faithfulness." Every day was a fresh canvas, an opportunity to experience the renewing aspects of God's love, calling him to lean into their embrace. He could start anew, regardless of yesterday's failures.

Yet, hope also required action. The Seeker understood that accepting God's eternal love necessitated an active response. He was called not only to receive love but to reciprocate it, to embody that love in his relationships with others. The words of Jesus resonated in his heart, instructing him to go forth and love as He had loved unconditionally and relentlessly. This charge prompted him to reflect on how he could manifest that divine love in practical ways, fostering connections that mirrored the acceptance he had received from God.

In a time marked by division, conflict, and pain, the Seeker wondered how a love that rises above human limits could become a powerful source of healing. He envisioned small acts of kindness rippling outward, creating waves of love that reached places he could not even fathom. This journey of living out love reached beyond his close circle; it called him to welcome and care for those who were different, overlooked, or lost. The Seeker recalled the parable of the Good Samaritan, a timeless lesson on radical compassion. He sensed a tug at his heart. This was not just about receiving love; it was a call to action, a reminder that God's love flowed freely to everyone, and it was his privilege to join that flow.

It was essential to establish a deeper understanding of the community as well. The Seeker reflected on the ways people could strengthen their bonds through love. The early church painted a beautiful picture of unity: "All the believers were one in heart and mind" (Acts 4:32, NIV). There was a divine power in gathering together, sharing burdens, and uplifting one another, a way to fully embody the essence of everlasting love. He recognized that he didn't have to walk his path alone; the beauty of God's design rested in connection, collective struggles, joyful celebrations, and mutual support.

As he sat there contemplating, the reality of God's love began to grow in his spirit. Everlasting love wasn't just an idea written in a book; it was a living force that shaped all of life. It was woven into everything, bringing purpose to ordinary moments, hope to hard times, and light to darkness. Each verse he internalized, every revelation he experienced, formed a protective sheath around his heart, fortifying him for the journey ahead.

The Seeker redirected his thoughts to those whose lives intersected with his own. Everyone represented a chance to reflect that divine love, sharing hope, encouragement, and kindness. Yet, he also recognized that pain intertwined with love; that there would be moments when love seemed far away. During those times, it was essential to return to the source, the promise of God's everlasting presence amidst grief and confusion. The beauty of such love was that it could dwell even in the valleys of despair.

With a heart warmed by the reflections of love that surrounded him, the Seeker felt invigorated. He decided to take a walk along the shore, letting the gentle lapping of the water remind him of the ebb and flow of life's rhythm. In every ripple, every wave crashing against the rocks, he heard a whisper: God's love persists. It transcends circumstances, wrapping around him like a soft blanket, ever-present and committed.

He felt a new resolve stirring within, one that beckoned him to draw near to God and invite others into that embrace. "Love is patient, love is kind" (1 Corinthians 13:4, NIV) echoed in his heart, guiding him to reflect on patience and kindness towards himself and others. He recognized that acknowledging his own struggles paved the way for understanding the struggles of those around him. In that essence, love became a shared journey, a path illuminated by vulnerability, humility, and grace.

As the sun sank further beyond the horizon, the sky was a transformation of twinkling stars. Each twinkle represented a promise, similar to the steadfastness of divine love, illuminating the night with hope. With renewed faith and understanding of God's abiding love, the Seeker left the shore that evening, mindful of the journey ahead.

He was ready to accept that promise, not only for himself but to share it freely with others. The journey of everlasting love was one to be experienced, nurtured, and celebrated. Above all, in his heart, the Seeker knew this was not just an ideal; it was the essence of life, the core of existence, and the very nature of God Himself. It was time to live in the fullness of that promise, allowing it to shape his every thought, action, and relationship. In doing so, he would become a vessel of God's love, reflecting its beauty and magnitude into a world that often thirsted for hope and connection.

Living in the Light of Eternal Love

Within the ever-changing landscape of uncertainty and fleeting moments, the idea of eternal love serves as a steadfast anchor. This concept offers a divine certainty that God's love is unfailing, limitless, and transformational, transcending the temporal joys and sorrows we experience. Our daily lives can be significantly impacted by living in the light of eternal love, which can greatly influence how we navigate our thoughts, actions, relationships, and ultimately, our purpose.

The Mentor sits with the Seeker under the arching branches of a flamboyant tree, a place where sunlight filters through the leaves in a warm cascade of light and shade. The atmosphere is rich with serenity, inviting contemplation and connection.

"My dear Seeker," begins the Mentor, "understanding God's eternal love is not merely a theological proposition; it is a life-altering realization. It invites us into a relationship that is deeply rooted in acceptance and grace. When we grasp that God's love is eternal, we are compelled to respond in meaningful ways."

The Seeker nods, feeling the weight of those words. "But how?" he asks earnestly. "How do I allow that understanding to influence my daily life?"

The Mentor smiles warmly, delighting in the opportunity to guide. "Let's explore this journey together, shall we? First, we must recognize that living in light of eternal love begins with an acknowledgment of our identity as beloved children of God. When we see ourselves through this lens, it transforms the narrative we tell ourselves."

The Seeker thought about this and realized that the noise of the world often tells a different story, one that makes people feel not good enough, like they must prove their worth through outside approval. Yet, as they sit in this sacred space, the truth of their identity as cherished by the Creator begins to resonate more profoundly.

"Your identity affects everything," the Mentor continues. "It influences your actions, your relationships, and the choices you make. Ask yourself, 'How would I act differently if I believed wholeheartedly that I am loved eternally by God?' This question opens the door to a remarkable shift."

As the Seeker reflects, the Mentor reemphasizes the practicality of this love. "Let's start with actions. When you know you are loved unconditionally, it becomes easier to extend that love to others. Think about the way you speak to people. Do you show kindness, patience, and empathy? Or do you reflect the world's harshness at times? The love you receive should spill over into the way you engage with the world."

The Seeker frowns for a moment, realizing the truth in this. It is often easy to mirror the negativity and anxiety present in society. However, he considered how delightful it would be to embody a love that reflects something far greater than mere human experience.

"Indeed," says the Mentor, sensing the Seeker's thoughts. "Consider your relationships. When you acknowledge God's eternal love, it cultivates an atmosphere of grace. You are more likely to forgive, to understand, and to support others because you understand your own need for grace. Envision approaching conflicts or misunderstandings with the heart of someone who has been forgiven countless times and chosen to love, regardless."

The idea of forgiveness arouses a memory in the Seeker's heart, a situation with a friend that had turned sour. He recalls the anger that once clouded his judgment. Could it be possible that by understanding God's eternal acceptance of him, he, too, could extend that love? Gradually, a shift begins within.

"Our choices, too," the Mentor continues, "are illuminated in the light of eternal love. When you perceive your decisions through the lens of love, the choices become clearer. You begin to ask, 'What would honor God? How would this action express love toward myself and others?' This can transform mundane moments into opportunities for divine expression."

The Seeker recalls instances of daily decision-making that often felt ordinary or even trivial. What if those moments were filled with intentionality and purpose rooted in eternal love? A simple choice to hold the door open for someone, to offer a smile to a passing stranger, or to take a moment to listen can carry the light of God's love.

"This awareness requires not just occasional reflection but a continuous practice," the Mentor advises. "Embrace spiritual disciplines that ground you in God's love—prayer, meditation, scripture reading, and community fellowship. These practices nurture a heart open to love and equip you to embody it. The more you engage with God, the more His love transforms you from the inside out."

As they engage in this dialogue, the Seeker feels the swell of inspiration. "I see now how living in light of eternal love can alter even the smallest interactions."

The Mentor's eyes twinkle, confirming the awakening within the Seeker. "Yes, and reflective questions can guide this transformation. Here are a few you may wish to meditate on:

1. How do I perceive God's love for me today?
2. In what ways can I express this eternal love to my family, friends, and community?
3. Are there areas in my life where I am withholding love or forgiveness?
4. What choices can I make that reflect my understanding of being loved unconditionally?
5. How can I cultivate awareness of God's presence as I go through my day?"

As each question lingers in the air, the Seeker jots them down in a small notebook, feeling the stirring of purpose within. He can sense that this journey will be ongoing, a lifelong exploration of living authentically in God's love.

"Moreover," the Mentor adds, "I encourage you to seek accountability within your community. Share your intentions with a trusted friend or join a group where love and support abound. This fosters an environment that encourages you to act upon your insights. Together, you can hold one another accountable, celebrate successes, and reflect on challenges."

The idea of group development resonates with the Seeker. He yearns to be a part of a community that values love over rivalry or judgment because he believes that there is strength in unity.

"Let me share a story," the Mentor says, leaning in closer. "There was once a man, let's call him Samuel, who lived with the shadow of self-doubt and shame. He had been hurt deeply in past relationships, which led him to build walls around his heart. One day, he came to understand that God saw him not as his past failures but as a beloved child, someone worth unending love. This realization ignited a flame within him.

"Samuel began to attend a community group focused on discussing faith and relationships. There, he shared his struggles openly, discovering vulnerability was a powerful expression of love. He started reaching out to others who were struggling, extending compassion borne from understanding. Each small act became a ripple effect of warmth and kindness in his community.

"Within months, Samuel observed a transformation, not only in himself but in those around him. As he lived in light of God's eternal love, a deep sense of purpose replaced his doubts. He found joy in serving others, spreading the message of love, and encouraging those who were still lost in their own battles."

The Seeker's eyes widen with realization. "Samuel found purpose through community, didn't he? His love for others blossomed from his understanding of God's love for him."

"Exactly!" the Mentor affirms. "Our journey in faith is often not meant to be a solitary one. When we embrace God's eternal love, we find ourselves drawn toward loving and serving others. It creates a chain reaction of grace that transcends individual lives."

With each passing moment under the flamboyant tree, the Seeker begins to see how possibilities unfold when they commit to living out their faith authentically. The beauty of God's love is that it is not a mere abstract concept; it breathes life into our everyday interactions and decisions.

"However," the Mentor notes, "the journey is not without its challenges. There may be days when you feel unworthy or unlovable, and that's okay. It is during these moments that you have the power to choose, return to God's promises, reaffirm your identity, and allow His love to wash over you again."

The Seeker leans back against the sturdy trunk of the tree, letting the cool breeze embrace him. "So, it's about more than simply understanding; it's about living it out consistently, even when it feels difficult."

"Precisely," the Mentor replies. "We are all works in progress. However, God's eternal love is a continuous invitation to begin again. Each day is a new chance to live authentically as children of God."

As the sun begins to set, casting golden rays across the landscape, the Seeker feels hope surging within him. "I want to harness this love, to embody it in ways that reflect God's heart."

"Then take these moments to reflect deeply on your actions and choices," the Mentor encourages. "Each decision you make can be a testament to the love you have received. Approach the world with open hands, ready to give and receive love generously."

With a renewed sense of purpose flooding his being, the Seeker takes a few last notes, capturing the essence of this transformative discussion. He realizes this step towards living in light of eternal love is not only a commitment to God but also to engaging wholeheartedly with those around him and fostering meaningful connections.

"I sense that expressing this love will create waves of transformation," the Seeker reflects. "And I yearn to share these reflections with others who may feel lost or burdened."

The Mentor smiles knowingly, "And that, my dear Seeker, is the heart of living in eternal love; it's about sharing the light you have received, illuminating the path for others to follow."

They sit together in silence for a moment, while the sky is painted with the golden hues of the sunset, serving as a stunning reminder of the beauty found in God's unending love. It encircles them, filling the voids left by uncertainty and doubt with hope.

As they prepare to leave this sacred place, the Seeker knows the journey has just begun. Equipped with insights, reflective practices, and the promise of eternal love, he steps forward into the world, ready to embody, reflect, and magnify the divine love that has forever changed his existence.

The journey of living in the light of eternal love isn't a one-time act; it's a daily commitment to honor the love we receive and share. In his heart, he feels a steady sense of purpose, a purpose deeply rooted in God's love, calling him toward growth, healing, and the joyful connection of community.

Hope and Assurance in God's Love

As we explore the concept of eternal love, we uncover a profound truth: God's love is not merely fleeting or conditional; it is everlasting, unshakeable, and remains constant throughout every season of our lives. In the turbulence of our existence, where uncertainty often looms large, the belief in God's eternal love serves as a beacon of hope and assurance. This love provides a wellspring of strength, comfort, and motivation for us to navigate the challenges we face.

The personal stories underscore a universal truth: God's love offers a tangible promise of assurance and hope for the weary, broken, and lost. It penetrates the depths of our despair, breathing new life into stagnant, wounded hearts. Such love invites us to step forward, not only embracing it for ourselves but also sharing it with the world around us.

As we reflect on these narratives, it becomes increasingly evident that the second step is to internalize how we can extend and share this gift of eternal love within our communities. When we truly understand how deeply God's love impacts our lives, we naturally want to share that love with others. It becomes both a calling and an invitation to take God's everlasting love and extend it to everyone around us.

Consider the beauty of a community that thrives on love and connection. We have the opportunity to inspire hope through outreach, service, and acts of kindness. Each small act of love communicates the message that no one is beyond the reach of God's affection. Just like the character in each story, we can become the hands and feet of God, bridging the gap between His eternal love and the ongoing struggles so many face.

Consciously seeking out those who feel lost, isolated, or burdened will allow us to foster an environment where God's love is both seen and felt. Volunteering at local charities, helping those in need, providing a listening ear, or simply offering a smile can create an impactful difference. Networking among friendships, neighborhoods, schools, and workplaces enables us to create spaces filled with love and acceptance, reflecting the heart of God.

As we embrace the challenge of sharing God's love, we must remember that every interaction is an opportunity for hope. It's in our small daily actions that we can provide individuals with the assurance they seek. We can remind them of their worth and help them see that just like us, they are loved and cherished unconditionally by the Creator of the universe.

Moreover, the act of sharing love does not solely extend to those we encounter in person. In this digital age, we hold the power to communicate God's message of eternal love through various platforms. Using social media, writing, or art can help spread our voices and share God's promises with more people. Every post and message can become a reminder of the hope we find in His love.

As we culminate this exploration of God's eternal love, let us not only reflect on the hope and assurance that come from understanding it but also commit to embodying this love in our lives. Acknowledging that we are recipients of grace should propel us into action as we strive to remind others that God's love knows no bounds.

The promise of God's eternal love brings hope in moments of turmoil, grief, and despair. When faced with challenges, we can lean into the assurance that no matter the circumstances, we are never alone. Our stories weave together a rich tapestry of faith, demonstrating that God's love is both an anchor in the storm and an invitation to generate hope within our communities.

Now, as we move forward, let's take this message of hope into the world. Let God's love change us so we can share that love with others. When we do, we help build connection, bring healing, and lift one another toward a brighter future filled with God's eternal promises. Together, we are called to spread hope and assurance, remind all of humanity that they are forever cherished by a loving God.

Conclusion

Thank you for the time we spent together.

Wow! Can you believe we've come to the end? It feels like just moments ago we were diving deep into the first chapter, but here we are, transforming together in the beauty of love like never before. First off, a huge heartfelt thank you for joining this journey. Your willingness to explore the depths of unconditional love signifies a bold step toward growth and community. We've explored our vulnerabilities, faced the challenge of forgiveness, and looked for ways to live out love in our daily lives. And let me say, having the courage to do this work is truly inspiring!

Remember, the essence of God's love is not a once-and-done concept. Oh no, it's an everlasting, ever-growing flame! You now possess tools, insights, and the invaluable wisdom that it is time for you to use, spread love like confetti in the world! Embrace the relentless pursuit of love in your life, starting today! And if you're feeling overwhelmed? Just remember that love is meant to be shared, and you're not alone on this journey.

I truly hope each chapter has left you feeling not just informed but activated! Take those reflective questions to heart. Use them to fuel self-discovery and open dialogues with others. Share what you've learned with your church or community, or even better, invite someone to join you on this journey. Love grows stronger when it's shared! Just as our personal experiences of love are important, so is the love we build within our churches and communities. Let's pull the insights we've gained from these pages into the world around us!

This journey has been marked by stories and testimonies that remind us we are all connected by our shared humanity. Each laugh, each tear, and every lesson is part of a grand medley of love that God has created. And hey, let's keep the conversations going! Connect with others, reflect on your experiences, and don't forget to challenge each other. As you nurture the love you've discovered, your journey will become part of a larger narrative, one that inspires future generations to embrace love as a way of life.

So as we part ways, take a deep breath and hold tight to the promise of God's everlasting love. Let it guide your actions, your words, and your heart. Whether you're being called to step into vulnerability, embrace forgiveness, or simply to love without borders, let your actions count in the days to come. The world is craving love, be the embodiment of it, and encourage others to do the same!

Thank you for allowing me to be a part of your journey. Remember, love isn't a destination; it's a continuous path we walk together. Until our hearts connect again, let's carry forth the echoes of divine love we've discovered. Keep spreading that beautiful, boundless love wherever you go!

With big, loving hugs,
Helen

www.ingramcontent.com/pod-product-compliance
Lightning Source LLC
Chambersburg PA
CBHW020324180726
47991CB00018B/590